# SILKY D BARES ALL

Matt!

Best Wishes
&
God Bless

'85

# Foreword

Dennis and I arrived together with the Bears in 1983. Generally, when a club drafts a wide receiver (Willie Gault) in the first round, you don't expect a free agent like Dennis to make the ball club.

But Dennis was just so clean. Watching him do what he was doing made me realize he was a better natural football player than Willie. Willie had world-class speed that stretched the field, but Dennis's presence gave Willie a lot of opportunities to make plays. Dennis was always hungry. When we were rookies down in the dungeon (the basement at Halas Hall), guys were talking a lot of trash. Sure, Dennis was talking his share, but he was also backing it up on the field. I always liked guys like Muhammad Ali and Reggie Jackson who could talk it up but back it up. Dennis was the same way.

Silky's value as a slot receiver was enormous. Dennis was tough, very, very tough. He wanted to prove that he had the talent, and he did. There were a lot of defenders in the NFL who were afraid of Dennis McKinnon. Silky was a complete, all-around player. Remember this, Gault could stretch the field, but Dennis was a complete football player.

--*"The Colonel" Richard Dent, Hall of Fame defensive end, 137.5 career sacks.*

In the pantheon of wide receivers, number 85 will live forever in the hearts of Chicago Bears fans who followed the fortunes of the team from 1983 to 1989. As an undrafted free agent out of Florida State, Dennis McKinnon displayed the heart, grit, and desire that helped the Bears win their only Super Bowl title back in 1985.

Dennis became a fan favorite and a favorite target for Jim McMahon because Mac knew he could always count on Dennis to make the big catch whether it was over the middle, an out route to the sidelines, or a deep ball to the end zone. I will never forget that Thursday night game at Minnesota in the historic year of '85. With the Bears reeling, down 17-9, Silky caught two touchdown passes, 25 and 43 yards to lead the Bears' comeback win over the Vikings. After the game Dennis treated his performance as just another day in the office during the post-game repartee.

I can guarantee you that Silky D will tell it like it is because he still tells it like it is. Dennis was a beast on the field and a gentleman off the gridiron. He continues to give back to the Chicago-area community with his words of wisdom for generations of young men who sorely need the guidance. You will not be able to put down Chet Coppock's look at the man I call my friend. Enjoy!

*--Jim Rose, Long-time sports anchor, WLS TV, Chicago.*

# Dedication

*To my beloved mom…all that I am today is built on the foundation that you laid out for me. You were my biggest fan. The basic values you taught me have earned me the respect and love of so many people. Soon I will join you in heaven, but right now, I know you know, I still have a great deal to accomplish. Mom, you know how much I love you and miss you.*

Dennis McKinnon  June 8, 2019

# Introduction

He was so gifted. Sadly, the Bears never utilized the passing catching skills of Dennis McKinnon as much as they should have. However, numerous former teammates of the mercurial Silky D stand in line to rave about his phenomenal blocking skills. I have been around the Bears for over 60 years, 50 of those as a reporter. I have always maintained that Dennis is the most underrated player in the 100 years of the NFL's most storied franchise.

I knew this book could not be a traditional read. Dennis's thought process moves too rapidly. We finally decided in late August 2018 how we wanted this to go. We would swap yarns and have conversations and tackle the issues of the day. Our regular hangout was a local restaurant/bar in north suburban Northfield. We laughed, and we talked about everything under the sun. I swear we talked about social and racial issues darn near as much as we talked the 100-yard war that is the NFL.

Welcome to my gab sessions with Silky D. You're in for one helluva ride.

*--Chet Coppock, 3/29/19*

Chet Coppock, tall and unapologetic. The velvet voice of versatility. I would talk to him and ask a question. He would start telling a story that had nothing to do with the question that I asked. He was so unique with a flair for the dramatic. His sudden passing leaves a scar on my heart that I will always carry. I love you big guy, thanks for your friendship and being a gift to me and so many others.

*--Dennis McKinnon 5/8/19*

# Chapter One

Trying to decipher Dennis Lewis McKinnon, a product of South Florida, can be a chore—for anybody. Sigmund Freud could have spent years with Dennis. Silky D is and always has been mercurial, on opinion overload, whether the topic is football, urban politics, or the cover of *Vogue Magazine*. We met on September 13, 2018 at a cozy restaurant near O'Hare Field to begin construction of our project. His smile remains electric—two parts Hollywood and one part the naughty eight-year-old boy who let the air out of your neighbor's tires.

If you go by the book, the unwritten NFL bible, which every team does, Dennis McKinnon had no business playing a single down of pro football. He was just too small. He was left out in the cold in the 1983 draft. After the '83 season, his knees fought him 24 hours a day, but his big heart and the prodigious chip on his shoulder far outweighed and out-fought the pain he felt daily during years when just walking could be a task. You just won't believe this, 182-pound Dennis McKinnon, at his peak, could leg press 800 pounds and squat 525, extraordinary numbers. Inch for inch, pound for pound, Silk was the strongest player on the Florida State Seminoles during his senior season.

I asked Dennis when he knew he had established himself as a rookie. "Probably about halfway through the year when I moved from the basement," he said. "We called it 'the dungeon.' I had to smell jocks in a grimy environment that was like an old attic. When I moved upstairs and saw myself sitting across Walter Payton, I knew I belonged."

He earned that promotion out of the dungeon the hard way.

"I loved the contact drills. During my first year in camp, our defense was testing us and trying to rough us up every day. At the time

I joined the Bears they were one of the NFL's charter franchises, but NOT a winning ball club. The Bears packaged 'greatness' around their history, but the 'monsters' I joined lacked a resume. With our contact drills, I got yelled at all the time during my rookie year. However, as I settled in, I noticed something. I could count the way guys lined up for the drill. There were clearly defensive players who didn't want to face me. Coaches also noticed that."

When Mike looked at Dennis, he saw himself as a rookie back in 1961 trying to impress owner-coach George Halas. Listen, Ditka weighed about 235 while Silk was rail thin, but their mentality was strikingly similar. They both wanted to rip heads off—literally.

"I don't know why I really loved contact as much as I did," Dennis says. "I can't give you a reason that can be explained by genetics. I just knew this, the art of blocking is learning how not to get hit. Contact made me feel alive. It let me know where I was and who I was. Defensive players love to puff up their chests and brag about how much they like to inflict pain and that's for real. My job was to eliminate the myth, and I did."

McKinnon was also willing to do something the defensive players were unwilling to do.

"If you wanna prove your manhood, try returning punts," he says. "You know guys are going to get a free shot at you. Sometimes they'll take the shot knowing full well they're going to draw a penalty. They don't care, they just want to lay the wood. My goal was to make sure guys knew from our first snap who I was and what they were going to be dealing with all afternoon. I never wanted to disappoint myself or, worse yet, disappoint my teammates or Mike Ditka."

Unlike some of his drafted teammates, McKinnon came in with a chip on his shoulder.

"I signed with the club in 1983 as a free agent out of Florida State. Somehow, the word had leaked that I'd only run a 4.8 in the 40. My gosh, I could walk a 4.8. My time was actually 4.35. I was pissed. I wasn't drafted. I didn't even qualify to be Mr. Irrelevant. I was down but my momma told me to go over to the U (University of Miami), which was across the street from our apartment, and show teams they had dropped the ball on me. I listened and I earned a spot in the toughest sports league in the world. I can't truly express the love I have for my mother.

The Bears sent Buddy Ryan, the club's defensive guru, down to scout me. Why? Beats me. Why did Buddy buy into me? I think he was able to look at me from the other side of the ball, the other side of the line of scrimmage. He saw my tenacity. So, I signed with the Bears as an undrafted free agent."

Being undrafted wasn't the origin of that chip on his shoulder. That was already there.

"Maybe part of the hostility I displayed as a blocker goes back to me not being featured as a primary receiving option at Florida State. I had so much to give to the 'Noles that was left on the table. But I knew with the Bears that while the glare of the spotlight was on Walter, it would eventually find its way to me because we were involved in so many plays together. My rep as blocker began to emerge in late '83 when the Bears began to rack up some wins, show a pulse. We won five of our last six games that year and knocked Green Bay out of the playoffs on the final Sunday of the season. My rep really locked in 1984. Guys knew I wasn't gonna screw around. I was going to bust people up. I knew from time to time off the first snap that there were defensive backs who just didn't want to face me. I was 180 pounds, I had to be fearless and believe me, I was fearless."

At that point, he certainly wasn't doing it for the money.

"My first deal in '83 paid $40,000 with a $5,000 signing bonus. I had to be the lowest paid guy on the ball club. But in the mid-1980s after the 'Brothers Invasion' hit the Bears with me, Dave Duerson, Willie Gault, Wilber Marshall, Mike Richardson, Sack Man Richard Dent, the Fridge, and a few others, the Bears vaulted from mediocre to ultra-prime time."

And Silky D was no bit player in that Bears transformation.

"When I think about my football career with the Bears, I like to believe I'm on the short list of players the club just doesn't win without. However, football doesn't define you as a man. I know what I accomplished on the football field. I know during my years that nobody blocked with the authority that I brought to the field. Blocking was so much a part of my identity. But the fans and especially the media tend to overlook the hard work guys like me put in to make other players look good. The press will pick and choose who they want to be the 'stars.' It's easier to write about a touchdown catch than it is to write about a clearing block 15 yards down field that gives Walter Payton 10 extra yards on a carry.

I think I was always an unsung hero. I wasn't controversial, but I was colorful. I'll always be colorful. That's who Dennis McKinnon was and is. When I think about playing at Soldier Field, I do have times where I feel like people have left me out of the conversation, but I also know that Mike Ditka, the toughest SOB in the valley, was my biggest fan."

### ###

Dennis speaks with such enormous pride and devotion about his mother, Josephine McKinnon, nicknamed "Bunch," the youngest child in a family of 12 kids. You know in a heartbeat that this was a splendid woman of grace, charm, and uncompromising decency.

Josephine drove a school bus for 30 years, but along the way she also provided her own kids with a book of knowledge on respect, proper conduct, and speaking your mind if someone or something was eating at you. Dennis was her baby, a baby who would go on to excel as an all-city, all-county, and all-state football player during his prep days at South Miami High School where, interestingly enough, the student body was about 70 percent Cuban.

"Mom's heart was so big," Dennis explains. "She taught us not to piss and moan when things didn't go our way. I lost Mama way too soon. She passed away during Valentine's Day week, 1996. It still breaks my heart that I never had the chance to say good bye. There were Valentine's Day cards I sent her, still on the dresser, unopened. That was crushing. Mom's heart just gave out. She had a significant heart murmur and eventually was beaten down by a heart attack. This was a lady up every morning driving her bus at 5:00 a.m. When I was at Florida State I know there were times Mama would send me forty bucks when she knew I was light. She'd be late paying a bill, but she cared about me.

Yes, I was a mama's boy.

After my mom died, I went into a deep depression, which lasted nearly two years. I did seek out counseling. I felt terrible, horrific guilt that I hadn't moved Mama to Chicago to stay with me. I felt I had failed my responsibility. There were times I just broke down and cried as I tried to sort out Mama's death with my therapist. But I also knew this: Mama loved hot weather. She would have hated winters in Chicago. She would have despised the temps in Januarys."

Obviously she was his biggest 24 karat gold football fan, right?

"Oh yeah. But I also know this is fact. Look back on my final two years in high school. I was all-conference, all-county, and all-state as a receiver. However, I also kicked off, did our punting, and returned kicks and punts. Darn right I was the Alpha Dog. But Mama saw the big picture: education. In my heart I believe she was far more gratified that I got a degree at Florida State than she was that I made the Bears as a no-name walk-on."

The picture Dennis paints of his old man, on the other hand, isn't a feel-good puff piece direct from the pages of *People Magazine*. It makes you wonder how he maintained any mental stability.

"Dad was 6'4" and weighed 240 pounds," Dennis says. "He had a presence about him. You never questioned him. I was afraid to question him. I was in fear of my dad. In the black culture, discipline can be very traumatic physically. I was whipped with a belt, electric wiring, or a switch from a tree, among other things. Dad would never offer any feeling of love. He'd tell me after he beat me to suck it up, go to my room, and go cry by myself. Mama was the one who would put her foot down and tell my dad when he was roughing me up, 'No more beatings today.' That's why growing up in our household was loving and respectful but also terrifying. Dad and I had our disagreements, which led to more appointments with his discipline."

As his son gained popularity, Dennis's father had an even harder time.

"Dad also struggled with 'royalty.' When I began to emerge as a football player he just didn't like people telling him how great his son was. He never attended one of my football games with the 'Noles. Not one! Mom and Dad divorced when I was 16, which only drove me farther apart from him. However, he found a way to break Mama's heart when I was at FSU. On my graduation day he showed up—he was invited—but he arrived with a date. Who does that? Who shows up at a family event with a date? I was so thrilled for my mom. Her baby was getting a degree, and he shows up with a date. What my dad did caused major friction with my mom, which really pissed me off. It would be years before we spoke again. I was filled with contempt for my dad."

The conversation turns to today's Bears. I pointed out to Dennis that today's Bears don't give a damn about the '85 champs. They don't know that for one given season you guys were probably the greatest football team ever assembled and certainly the greatest group of characters ever assembled. What's more, they don't care.

"I also include the Bears' fan base in this picture," Dennis adds. "Even with Google walking them through what we accomplished, so many of our fans are clueless to history. We're treated like animals in the zoo by the contemporary players. Today's generation has money handed to them. How much money did the Bears toss out to sign wide receivers that weren't even starting for other teams? These kids don't want to hear about us. They just don't get it that the old school is about knowledge and wisdom. It's completely lost on today's player.

When I played, you stayed on the field until your hands were bleeding. That's what we were all about in the 80s. Today's guys all wear lipstick. We relished contact. Unless you saw blood, you played. When guys play bad today, they don't get called out and they should be called out. (Mike) Ditka used to call us out on the field and in the press all the time.

Why do you have so many guys with soft tissue injuries? Go back to training camp. Next-to-no hitting, very little running. Most of these guys aren't in shape. You saw at the beginning of the season. Why did (Matt) Nagy have the regulars sit out the third and fourth exhibition games? Fourth I'll give him. That's a waste of time to see who grabs the $51^{st}$, $52^{nd}$, and $53^{rd}$ spots on your roster. But (D-lineman) Akiem Hicks was sucking wind at the beginning of the year. Why didn't the Bears blitz the hell out of Rogers in the first game when he was playing on one leg? They weren't in shape.

This is simple. How do you develop success if you don't practice? Cosmetic shape isn't football shape. To play football the right way you need to absorb contact in August. Your body, your muscle memory has to be reawakened."

Silly D can offer up a Hollywood smile that could light up Las Vegas Boulevard, but these are subjects that elevate his anger level—big time. This is only one of them. He remains enraged that blacks have not made more progress within America's societal structure. He spits in the face of those athletes who have cowardly attacked a woman. A brooding expression will emerge as Dennis talks about cops beating up young blacks for no apparent reason or profiling blacks of any age. We will tackle all of those subjects and more, but for this day, and this lunch, it's time to call for the check.

# Chapter Two

By 1984, second-year man Dennis McKinnon was beginning to raise eyebrows around the NFL. That leads us to Don Pierson, a tremendous football writer. I've known Don, a long-time *Tribune* scribe with a huge passion for track and field, since we were both hanging around Soldier Field when the Bears were practicing regularly at the lakefront mortuary back in 1971. Don's cogent reporting along with his designs on getting the story right left an indelible impression on me. Ted told Pierson, who was writing for a different publication, that Dennis's blocking ability was "devastating."

Mike Ditka told Pierson, "Nobody does it better (blocking—than McKinnon). Nobody."

Ted Plumb was one of the coaches on the Bears, and he watched them day in and day out in practice, in the games, and on film. He had a definite opinion on #85.

"Willie Gault had great talent, but he didn't figure that blocking was in his contract. I'm not knocking Willie—he was a speed guy who just assumed that his job was just to get open. Willie was not tough physically. He was a track man playing football. That's just the truth. Gault was the fastest guy in the league. On the other side, Dennis would knock your ass off. I demanded that my guys use some basketball skills on the field. Maybe eight, nine times out of 10 you're not going to actually have to hit anybody, but you're setting a screen just by keeping a defender occupied. I told my receivers to play the game inside out. Remember, 9 times out of 10 the play is dead before contact is needed. Given their different skill sets, I had to coach Dennis one way and Willie a whole different way as we prepared for our next opponent. Dennis may well be the toughest guy I've ever been around mentally and, yes, he was the most underrated player on our Super Bowl Bears."

When I told Dennis what his former coach said, he was flattered.

"I had more responsibilities to our offense, especially in the run game. In this game we love to play, you have to be smart and that is certainly one of the many qualities I inherited playing for Ted Plumb."

I take the conversation back to '84 and the NFC title game. The Bears got trounced by Frisco 23-nothing in the NFC title game at Candlestick Park.

"It was just a strange week all the way around," Dennis recalls. "We had beaten the Redskins in D.C. to advance. We left early for Northern California because we didn't have an indoor facility in Lake Forest. Our offense just had no rhythm, and we went into the lion's den without our tiger. McMahon was hurt so Steve Fuller was our quarterback. With Mac, it didn't matter what play was sent in from the sidelines. Jim ran what he damn well pleased, so we weren't shackled from the bench. Fuller stayed with the script. Our pre-snap adjustments, audibles, and other elements were gone.

The Niners not only beat us, they insulted us. We were bullied. Then to make matters worse, O'Hare had weather trouble, so we had to stay in the Bay Area overnight. The next morning *The San Francisco Chronicle* just chewed us up. We got shutout and the *Chronicle* was determined to let the whole world know it.

There was only one bonus. I got a playoff check."

###

After the arugula salad arrives, the conversation shifts once again to the modern Bears. Dennis has a healthy respect for 2018 pickup Khalil Mack, but he cautioned against getting overexcited.

"I could game-plan against Khalil Mack just by watching him on TV," Dennis opines. "You gotta make Mack cover guys. Keep him moving. Send a guy in motion to his side or throw a screen pass. Right now he's just bull rushing, which guys are far more comfortable doing today than they were back when I played for one reason: they don't have to worry about getting cut blocked. You get cut blocked and you mentally hesitate when rushing to sack the quarterback."

I wonder what Dennis thinks about Mack's football IQ.

"I can't tell you how cerebral Mack is because he doesn't have to worry about playing the run or dropping into coverage. He has one job—rush the passer. Mack's primary job is to be disruptive and record sacks. Every now and then he will drop into coverage, but that's not his strength. Offenses have to send motion guys at him, chip him, or double-team him. Yes, he's that good.

I will say this. If I had to make a choice—one game winner-take-all—I'd go with Mack over Brian Urlacher. Brian was a great side-to-side linebacker, but you could beat him straight up. Right now, Mack is carrying the Bears' defense."

I wonder how he compares to the linebackers on Silky's Bears team.

"Today, with the rule changes, outside rushers can rush the passer without hesitation because you can't cut a defender outside the tackle box. The league has made an effort to protect guys' knees, so sack stats are up across the league. Put it this way, back in '85 when we won the Super Bowl, teams didn't game-plan for (Mike) Singletary, they game-planned against Wilber Marshall."

How does Khalil fit into the rest of the defense, I ask him.

"Khalil has been around. He knows one thing right now. He's a marked man. Defensive coordinators have to game-plan for Mack. They don't have to game-plan for Leonard Floyd (former first round pick out of Georgia). One guy has given the Bears defense a charge this year: Khalil Mack. Without Mack, you're basically back to running 2017's defense and a 5-11 record.

The Bears are paying Mack 141 million dollars. He's the highest-paid defensive player in the league. Will Mack accept a cortisone shot? I doubt it. We all did back in '85, but Mack doesn't have to prove anything to anybody. He's living on enough guaranteed money to feed four generations of Mack family members.

It's interesting to watch how the media operates in Chicago, where fans cling to any shred of hope with the Bears. Bears fans and the media will look at all the positives, but hardly spend any time looking at the negatives. A young team can only get better when it learns from its mistakes. Even Stevie Wonder can see we aren't a great team yet, but we are more competitive than we have been in probably a decade.

The Bears have to keep Mack healthy. He is their identity."

### 

The schism! Offensive players on the '85 Bears have justifiable resentment towards the guys on the defensive side of the ball. Why? Because the Buddy Ryan-led "D" grabbed most of the headlines and radio talk show time. Yes, the defense was prolific, dangerous, maniacal, and overwhelming, but that defense was also given plenty of downtime due to an offense that led the NFL in rushing and in time of possession. Even today, nearly 40 years after the glory of winning Super Bowl XX, most of the offensive players on that majestic '85 team feel they've been short-changed.

Dennis's eyes light up when he recounts tales of the days the offense bested the defense. The stars of this story are "Mongo" McMichael, who was from a different solar system, and Jimbo Covert, who is almost certainly the best left tackle who's not sporting the gold blazer (size 52-XXXL?) from the Pro Football Hall of Fame. Big Jim is the only member in the NFL's 1980 All-Decade team not enshrined in Canton, Ohio.

Jimbo and I once appeared on the same wrestling card at the Rosemont Horizon (now the All State Arena). This goes back to 1986 and WrestleMania II. I was one of the ring announcers for the card and to this day still get chills when I think about introducing The Fabulous Moolah and a world-class dummy billed as Brutus "The Barber" Beefcake. Anyway, Covert appeared on the show as part of an historic(?) 20-man over the top Battle Royale along with William Perry. Jimbo, a two-time All-American at Pitt, a tremendous amateur wrestler and weight lifter, suffered a terrible humiliation during the "Royale." He was flipped over the top rope by the legendary King Tonga roughly 30 seconds into the "Royale Smash." Of course, Covert suffered terrible emotional trauma(???), but Jim later told me it was the easiest 35 grand he ever made in his life.

"You know Steve was always running his mouth and disrespecting the offense," Dennis says about Mongo, relishing the opportunity to tell the story. "It didn't make a damn bit of difference that we led the league in rushing four straight years. The defense always treated us like dirt. During 7-on-7 drills and 9-on-7 drills they tried to take the heads off our offensive line. Again, you know Mongo can't shut the hell up. Our defense tried to create the feeling that the offense wasn't worth two cents.

Yes, there were times I wanted to ask Hampton (who signed with the Bears in 1979) and maybe Otis (Wilson, joined the Bears in 1980), what did you guys win before the class of '83, Gault, Double D, Covert, Mike Richardson, Mark Bortz, Jay Hilgenberg, and myself? The fact is they didn't win shit before the '83 guys showed up.

I'll never forget the day Jimbo went up against McMichael in practice. He just crushed Mongo. He jacked him up, pounded him, and sat on him while the offense cheered. That was the day our offense gained and won respect."

###

This has to be mentioned. Veteran's Day is coming up and I figured Silky and I would break bread as we continue our "journey." Fahgedaboudit! I didn't realize it was the day for honor and observance.

Every Vet's Day, asking for no fanfare, no applause, seeking no recognition, Silky spends a 12-hour day visiting with those who have served, those who have lost limbs, those who feel as if society has left them out in the cold. Far too many who think society just doesn't give a damn if they're alive or dead. You're damn right I admire the guy who wore jersey 85 for the Chicago Bears.

"I was one of three brothers." Dennis explains one of the reasons he is drawn to this day. "My older brother Terry was a prolific artist; he loved to draw. Terry elected to forego a college scholarship to study art in order to join the Army. He served for over 30 years and was in combat in the Gulf War and Desert Storm. Terry rose to the rank of Master Sergeant.

My younger brother, Jeffery, was very short; he inherited my mom's height. He sometimes didn't get the attention he deserved, but his heart is as big as hearts can be. Me? I inherited Mom's dimples and her smile. I was always in trouble with my dad. I questioned everything and inherited the McKinnon stubborn gene."

That stubborn gene has served Silky D well. So has his big heart. I have so many questions to ask him about both of those attributes, but they will have to wait for another day.

Silk exits into his gleaming "baby" Hummer with rims so big you think they could fit a 747. We will meet again in seven days—maybe less. There's just so damn much to talk about.

# Chapter Three

On paper Dave Duerson at age 45 appeared to be the very essence of the American dream. A splendid athlete at Muncie Northside High School, about 60 miles northeast of Indianapolis, Double D went on to become a two-time All-American at Notre Dame while graduating with honors. His NFL career with the Bears included four consecutive Pro Bowl appearances, 1985 thru '88, along with two All Pro selections. Dave was also chosen NFL Man of the Year in 1987.

Now, jog your memory, do you recall that while winning a Super Bowl in 1985 with the Bears, Due also picked up another ring with the Giants in 1990?

His business success was hardly a revelation. Dave was an exceptionally bright man who at one time ran Duerson Foods, a meat packing company, in southern Wisconsin that was supplying breakfast patties to McDonalds and Burger King and Swedish meatballs to Olive Garden.

"Dave appeared to be an All-American boy," Dennis explains, "but if you knew him, really knew him, you understood he had obsessive compulsive disorder. You have to remember, he lost his spot on the Notre Dame board of trustees at Notre Dame, a position he treasured, after an altercation with his wife Alicia. He also had several business failings. When I was working the meat business with him, I began to notice a change in Dave's personality. Among other things, he was either late or would completely forget about meetings. I'd tell him I'm here with clients, where are you? When he relocated to Sunny Isles (Florida), I think he really just wanted to be alone."

February 17, 2011, Duerson, lying in his bed in his Florida residence, pulled the trigger on a handgun and ended his life. Yet he didn't depart without a significant statement. Even in death, Dave saw a way to help his football brethren. He messaged his family to have his brain shipped to the Boston University School of Medicine, which was doing extensive work on the effects of CTE.

"It was criminal the way Dave was portrayed in the movie *Concussion*," Dennis says now. "Evidently, Hollywood felt it needed a bad guy, a villain, so they cast a deceased Dave Duerson in that role. Here's the point. Dave was a trustee with the NFLPA on the Benefits Committee. As you recall, in the film, he is displayed as uncaring ex-player who is basically telling Andre Waters, the former Eagle, that he has no interest in helping Andre collect any benefits."

Waters also checked out early. Racked by depression, Andre shot himself to death on November 20, 2006. A neuropathologist in Pittsburgh determined that brain damage from playing football had left Andre with the brain of an 80-year-old man.

"You know Dave was on the board directors of the NFLPA, our union. There were many times he rejected requests from ex-players, but the way he was shown in the film was completely unfair. Dave was just one man on the board. *Concussion* got it right with Mike Webster, the Steelers' Hall of Fame center. He was living out of a truck. Terry Bradshaw, his old teammate, was sending him money on a regular basis. The poor guy was helpless."

Try and figure this one out. Media knew Mike Webster was already brain damaged, determined as disabled before, BEFORE, he left the NFL. With the passage of time, Mike's brain became nothing more than glorified oatmeal.

"You're darn right I can be upset with the NFL for its lack of responses with so many players who have suffered," Dennis says. "So many players have never seen a dime from the NFL's so-called concussion settlement. But I am really disgusted with our union because our leader DeMaurice Smith just doesn't fight for the retired players. Neither did Gene Upshaw, our leader before Smith. I wasn't sure if Upshaw was on the player side or on the owner's payroll.

I wish the Hollywood producers of *Concussion* would have called me. I had so much to offer that would have made the film more relevant and realistic. Dave was my friend, my brother. I knew him as well as anybody. Double D and I came in together. We first hooked up in '82 when my Florida State team beat Dave and Notre Dame in South Bend. I remember The Irish left the grass as high as possible to try and slow our guys down. But Due and I really bonded when we both came to Chicago in the summer of '83.

The atmosphere at rookie camp in June of 1983 was a little strange unless you were there. The heat in our dorms was unbearable, and of course, we had no air conditioning. I remember Dave and I and some of the other rookies, guys like Richard Dent and Mike Richardson, got a lift over to a Kmart off Route 41, and we bought what seemed like every single electrical fan in the place. Guys would be walking around butt-naked in the dorms, it was so hot. We had no amenities, no AC. You learned about life in the NFL in a hurry. Until you made the ball club, you were roadkill. Most guys didn't have cars and we had no clue how to ride the train or hop the bus. All we wanted to do was find the bright lights of Chicago. Of course, we had to sing for our meals. That was all part of being a rookie."

Let me squeeze in a note about Dave Duerson. Back in 1987, I was chosen "Man of the Year" by the Italian American Sports Hall of Fame, a pretty neat trick given that I'm a bohunk. I gave a great deal of thought to who I wanted to present me for the honor. Finally, I decided on Double D. When I called him and asked him to help me, he told me he was going to be in New York and wouldn't be able to make it. Then there was a three or four second pause. Due said, "Chet, don't worry, I'll hop on an early flight for you."

"He truly wanted to help out people who really needed help," Dennis adds. "I used to love to travel with Due to Muncie, where he established a foundation to help people with alcohol and drug problems. Double D wasn't looking for headlines. Dave was such a humble man with tremendous intelligence. You know intelligent brothers remain a threat to segments of white culture."

And yet he had an impact on the league and future players in ways that still aren't completely understood or appreciated.

"The death of Dave Duerson forced the NFL to examine CTE," Dennis says. "You wouldn't see those blue concussion protocol tents on the sidelines if Dave hadn't taken his own life. After the shock of Dave taking his own life at his home in Florida, I cried. I hurt. It also still hurts me that I wasn't asked to be a pallbearer or speak at his funeral. His wife Alicia shut me out. I loved Dave. I always will. He was my brother in so many different ways. His legacy in death is that the league is safer for today's NFL player. Moms have more interest and say-so in their sons playing football or avoiding the game. Today's players owe a debt of gratitude because he forced the league to do what's right.

The former Arizona Cardinal Pat Tillman died of friendly fire while serving in Afghanistan. The story was initially reported that Tillman was struck by the enemy. You know the league gives the Pat Tillman Foundation a small fortune every year. Just what do they do for the Dave Duerson Foundation? What do they really do for the Walter and Connie Payton Foundation? The answer? No real money."

Silky realizes that age 60 is creeping up on him. I ask him about his own condition, his own fears.

"I admit that I do have days when I think about it (CTE), but I believe I was handed a winning lottery ticket. I know my brain is sharp and my memory is intact. Also, I'm blessed that my body, despite the wear and tear of the game, is in very good shape. I don't have any doubts about my intelligence. I've always been a quick study. That hasn't changed. You know, I never wanted to be on the bench. The bench is for losers. The bench to me seemed like a jail sentence. I was sent to war without a great deal of major equipment, it was the 80s, and I feel blessed that I'm in good shape today, some 30 years since I last played. I do worry about some guys on our '85 club. I won't name names, but I am concerned about all of our offensive linemen and our trio of linebackers, Otis, Mike, and Wilber—Cadillac linebackers. You know some people think Richard Dent has brain trauma, but that's not the case. Richard just talks at a very slow pace, so people make incorrect assumptions.

Believe me, all retired players have CTE lurking in the back of their minds."

###

Dennis is a flamboyant guy, but he also deals in reasonability. As the subject turns to the modern-day Bears, he sums up his opinion in one sentence.

"I'm not sold on the Bears—not yet."

To set the stage, the rest of Chicago was positively giddy at that moment. The Bears were basking in a 48-10 win over a team advertising itself as the Tampa Bay Buccaneers when in fact it might have been the Highland Park Little Giants or the Mount Carmel Caravan. Despite the big win, there was a moment that bothered Dennis. Akiem Hicks got into a minor scrum with Tampa guard Ali Marpet. The contact occurred when down judge Mike Carr decided to try and separate the two players. Hicks made contact with Carr and got tossed out, but that was just the warm-up act. Akiem tossed his shoulder pads and jersey into the stand for reasons best known to Akiem Hicks. Remarkably, Hicks wasn't suspended for his lunacy but was given the NFL minimum fine of just over 33,000 dollars for behavior that falls under the category of childish.

"You know what I'd tell Hicks about that play?" Dennis poses the rhetorical question. "You got a mulligan. You should have been suspended. The Bears have some momentum for the first time in years, and the club could have lost you for its next game at Miami, a tough place to play because of heat and humidity. I'd also tell Hicks you make about one play a quarter and throw your arms up in a celebration. If Nagy called out Hicks for what he did, I don't think Akiem would quit on the coach. Nagy can talk to him privately, but he'd be making a mistake if he called out Hicks in front of his teammates."

A few weeks later Hicks was once again the topic of our conversation. Hicks was inserted into the ballgame in a goal line situation by Matt Nagy. Hicks scored from a yard out.

"Nagy was showboating when he put in Hicks," McKinnon says. "Let me tell you, if I'd been a New York d-lineman I would have gone right for his knees because you're trying to make me and my guys look bad. You're trying to make me look real bad. You're insulting us."

There's a great differentiation between the Hicks touchdown and the famous plunge by Fridge in 1985. Fridge was the rare 300-pound NFL football player. People loved his gap-toothed grin. Fridge got press immediately when Buddy Ryan called him a wasted draft choice. William ran over Green Bay linebacker George Cumby on Monday Night Football to break the plane and Cumby's spirit. And Fridge became an instant celeb.

"You left out one piece," Dennis says. "William also wasn't a starter at the time. He was just a role player. Buddy Ryan was still calling him '72' instead of his name."

The William Perry story doesn't have a happy ending. William was used by family, so-called friends, agents, and hangers-on. He's in very bad shape. I pray for him. Behind that gap-toothed grin that made him so cuddly, there was a very complex person who really detested the limelight.

Fridge is a very sick man. Some think he has rudiments of CTE. We know he still drinks and eats like he's going to the joint. The ex-Clemson All-American is brutally obese. His financial picture makes you wonder what he did with all those 25,000 paydays for cutting ribbons at shopping centers or appearing in McDonald's TV spots. Remarkably, this is a guy I once saw do a standing slam-dunk of a basketball. I'm dead serious.

"William is a great guy," Dennis says. "A great teammate. Let me tell you what Fridge did. As a rookie football player, a role player if you will, he clogged the middle and elevated the play of Steve McMichael. Plus, this will surprise you, Perry made Mongo concentrate to a greater extent on the field. People just don't know what a great athlete a young William Perry was. Remember, William was running downfield on kickoffs as a wedge buster. Imagine this guy, a physical freak, coming at you full speed on a kickoff.

You know the media can suck the life out of a ball player, and it did so with Fridge. The press, the TV cameras, can bite you. Fridge didn't know how to handle the media, and he really had no interest in dealing with the press. Think about Mike Ditka ignoring Walter and allowing Fridge to score that made-for-TV touchdown in Super Bowl XX. You think Ditka wasn't thinking about marketing and showmanship? Listen, Ditka made money off the brothers on the Bears. The NFL doesn't want to address issues that make the league look bad. When Fridge was an entertainer and his name was selling merchandise, the league embraced him. Now the NFL doesn't give a damn if he lives or dies."

###

The subject of Dennis's father comes up again in conversation, and after what he has previously told me, I'm a little surprised to hear they are still in contact. How did they get back on track?

"When I lost Mama, I was devastated," Dennis says. "I have never gotten over her death. It's still surreal to me that she's not around. I knew, I just knew, that Mom wouldn't be at peace if Dad and I didn't reconcile. So I reached out and we began to communicate. We talk all the time now, not just for Mom, but for the importance of the McKinnon legacy."

We still have much more to explore about the McKinnon legacy, but it will have to wait for another day. The busboy is eyeing our table. The chilly Northfield air awaits us as we make plans for a follow-up visit.

# Chapter Four

I've asked Dennis to name his top 10 NFL players over the past 35-40 years. Naturally, he comes up with 12 and leaves plenty of room for genuine bar room arguments. No surprise on the first name.

"Tom Brady changes the temperature in the room," Dennis says. "He allows his teams to be at peace mentally. Tom has taken every test and knows all the answers. Over the years, Brady has probably elevated the value of the Patriots what? Eight or nine hundred million bucks. And you have to admire this. The guy has taken pay cuts over the years to help the Patriots fit players under the cap."

I point out his abilities as a play caller.

"More often than not Tom Brady doesn't call a play in the huddle," Dennis points out. "He just calls a formation. By the way, Brady handles the pre-snap read far better than Peyton Manning ever did. Brady will eye the defense as his offense sets up. He's been around for so many years he almost knows, based on experience, how the D is going to approach him. Brady will call a play and then begin making adjustments if there's time left on the play clock."

I ask Silky if Belichick makes Brady better or vice versa.

"Try this on," Dennis says. "Bill Belichick would be just another coach without Tom Brady. Gronk (Rob Gronkowski) wouldn't have been Gronk without Brady. Last season Gronkowski was no longer a major red zone component for the Pats. For years inside the 20, he was to New England what Jason Whitten was to Tony Romo in Dallas or Antonio Gates was to the Chargers' Phillip Rivers. Gronkowksi became primarily a blocker for the Patriots. He took up space, he loved to hit people. That's the New England mentality: we're gonna bust you up. At one time, you could look at Gronk and say, yes, he represented points on the board."

I ask Silk if there's a certain type of player that Brady likes.

"Brady needs players who are cerebral, guys who will go nuts looking at film. That's why Chad Ochocinco (Chad Johnson—766 career catches) was a bust in Foxboro. He didn't put forth the work ethic to stand side-by-side, work in tandem with, Brady. Chad couldn't master the Pat's playbook and he just couldn't read defenses. Brady is throwing to Clydesdales, not stallions. Tom doesn't have burners. That takes skill in today's NFL, where everything is about speed and Fantasy Football points."

Finally, I ask Dennis if Tom Brady would have put up anywhere near the numbers in the 1980s that he's put up for Bill Belichick.

"Absolutely not," Dennis admits. "Teams never ran with five wide in my era. But I will give Tom credit for this. I can't think of anyone who has evolved with the game like he has. Spygate, Deflategate, who cares? Brady is always one step ahead of the NFL's next confusing rule change."

The next one on Silky's all-time great list is a fellow wide receiver.

"Jerry Rice," he says without hesitation. "He's the best-conditioned athlete I've ever seen. Walter Payton ran 'The Hill,' that steep incline near his home in the northwest suburbs. Jerry took conditioning to a new level. This is a fact. Jerry made (Joe) Montana better than he actually was. Was he arrogant? Of course, wide receivers have to be arrogant. Rice took care of business unlike a guy like Dez Bryant. Dez put up big numbers with the Cowboys, but what did Dallas win with him? At the end of '17, the club couldn't wait to get rid of him. Bryant is a classic example of great talent gone south. Rice was always sleek, fashionable on the field. He lived off the Deion Sanders code: if you look good and feel good, you play good."

Silky's greatest running back of all-time is also not a surprise.

"Walter Payton," he says, naming his most famous ex-teammate. "People forget about the fact that Walter had no upfront protection or passing game during his first five or six years with the Bears. The wear and tear on his body was overwhelming since clubs knew the Bears couldn't throw the ball and loaded eight guys in the box. Don't forget this: Walter played his entire career on that terrible Astroturf at Soldier Field. That took an enormous toll on his body. Walter had to carry the load by himself for so many years with the Bears. No matter what anybody says, the Bears 46 defense didn't become great until Richard Dent, Dave Duerson, and Mike Richardson arrived in '83 and Wilber Marshall in '84. How much winning were (Dan) Hampton, Otis (Wilson), and Mongo (McMichael) doing before '83? The answer is not much."

What about on the defensive side of the ball? Who was the greatest?

"Lawrence Taylor," Dennis replies. "People ask how intelligent L.T. was about the game of football, and I tell them how intelligent do you have to be when your only job is to seek and destroy? When he busted Joe Theismann's leg on Monday Night Football back in 1985, Lawrence became infamous. Theismann never played again. It was intimidating just watching L.T. on 8-millimeter film."

I know Lawrence got swept up by the New York glitter, Studio 54, and stuff like that, but hear me out. This guy was a household name bigger than the governor, bigger than the mayor. Everywhere he goes he's a guest. People won't let him go anywhere near a check, and those people are frequently carrying the goodies. Lawrence was always on his red carpet.

"You wanna know how good I was?" Dennis says. "Ask Lawrence Taylor. In the first game of the '85 playoffs (actually January 1986), we beat New York 21-0. We were in their heads. I caught a pair of TD passes from Jim McMahon in that game. We ran our flop-wing, motion slide slant, 37 sweep. L.T. had to know that when I went in motion to the left that 80 percent of our plays were going to be sweeps with me as the lead blocker for Walter (Payton). I waited for Lawrence to pursue and I just busted him right below his ribcage. My first reaction (laughter) was I should help him up. Keep a few things in mind. There is no linebacker in the NFL today who is the total package that L.T. was. Nobody. Two, after I nailed Lawrence, my teammates were laughing at L.T. and laughing along with me."

Did Lawrence get angry?

"He was pissed. How pissed off was L.T? On the next play he lined up right in front of me. This is the baddest guy in the valley, the head of the snake. That told me I had gotten inside his head. No, we did not shake hands after the game, but I have seen L.T. a few times over the years while working with Gridiron Greats. We've been cordial. L.T. and I do get along. However, because of that block I put on L.T., we are in a way forever linked. Part of my job was to create fear beyond our offensive line. And I did that! That play seems so far in the past—back when the NFL was fun. You know you could try and game-plan for L.T., but it just didn't work that way. He lined up wherever he wanted. The guy was such a presence. Lawrence was a complete football player. Guys like Julius Peppers and Von Miller are guys with talent, but guys who play on passing downs. The game is no longer about tackles. It's not about full stats. It's all about sacks."

I was surprised that Aaron Rodgers didn't make Silky's list, but there was another Packer who did.

"Brett Favre," Dennis says. "I give Brett a slight edge over Aaron Rodgers because Brett was special. He was a football player. He loved contact. Favre, while being the face of the league back in the 90s into the new millennium, also got banged up a lot. He was just as good as

(John) Elway throwing across his body. Brett threw lasers across his body. Both guys, Aaron and Brett, were and are very mobile. Look at Rodgers. Do you think Randall Cobb or Jordy Nelson rate as truly great receivers? No, they were good, but Rodgers' ability to extend plays made them appear to be great. I'd love to play just one year in this era with Brett. We'd put up huge numbers."

Another name on Silky's list is a fellow Seminole.

"Deion Sanders," he says. "Prime was always the fastest guy on the field—always. I give him an edge as the best. I give him a slight edge over Bo Jackson as the best pure NFL athlete—note, athlete—I've ever seen. The Cowboys don't win a Super Bowl in '95 without Deion. Prime made the game entertainment. You gotta love a guy who genuinely believes he can change field position."

Deion isn't the only defensive back on Silky's list.

"Ronnie Lott," he says. "Another great athlete out of USC. His preparation was as intense as his play on the field. The Niners D was about Ronnie Lott. He was the best player on the back end of a defense you could ever hope to see. Lott would tell you he never avoided danger."

Four more greats on Silky's list are all Hall of Famers, or soon will be.

"Barry Sanders. I genuinely believe he retired to avoid breaking Walter Payton's NFL record for rushing (since surpassed by Emmitt Smith, 18,355 career yards). Barry was within striking distance of Sweetness. He left the Lions about 1,300 yards shy of Walter. Randy Moss could jump out of the gym and he ran a 4.2. He made the deep ball poetic. Reggie White was the consummate pro. The Minister of Defense. He prayed before he hit you. He didn't care about double-teams. Reggie was blessed with a great motor. Green Bay doesn't win a Super Bowl in January of '97 without White. There was an aura of respect about him that traveled wherever he went. Rod Woodson played

17 years. He fascinated me when he was with the Steelers. Rod holds the NFL record (32) for fumble recoveries by a defensive player and interceptions returned for touchdowns (12). He was also a long jumper at Purdue."

The final name on Silky's list was another ex-teammate.

"Wilber Marshall is the most underrated player in NFL history. The fact that he's not in the Hall of Fame along with Jim Covert and Jay Hilgenberg illustrates the east coast bias, the resentment against the Bears. Wilber is the best player not in the Hall. The guy was brisket burnt on both ends—succulent on the inside and very dark on the outside. When (Mike) Singletary got a deal with the Bears assuring him he'd always be the club's highest-paid linebacker, it drove Wilber nuts. Wilber knew, we all knew, that Singletary was the club's in-house informant."

Marshall was a Swiss Army knife. Tell me any defensive player in the NFL at 225 pounds who played on the same level as Wilber? Why did Marshall leave the Bears for the free agent payday with the Redskins? He just didn't believe the Bears respected him enough.

I asked if any current players (other than Brady) should make the list.

"No, I'm not going to list a Gronkowski or J.J. Watt now. Let's see them play a few more years before we pass judgment."

### 

The discussion about Lawrence Taylor takes my brain back to that playoff game after the 1985 season. My memories of that game run very deep. To such an extent that the Bears excellence against Bill Parcells and New York seems more vital to me than the team's Super Bowl win over New England 21 days later. Hear me out. I recall walking along the sidelines with sportscaster and ex-football player Mike Adamle about 90 minutes before kickoff time. The Soldier Field carpet had no cushion: it was just a crowned slab of Astroturf that was as unforgiving as the pavement on the Eisenhower Expressway. The temperature was miserable, just slightly above zero, but that wasn't the real villain, the villain dressed in black. A savage wind out of the northeast was running at about 18 miles per hour. It was the kind of weather that makes your eyes tear while your cheekbones begged for a fireplace.

The "Old Grey Lady," *The New York Times*, reported the wind chill at 13 below. My own guess is it was closer to 20 below. Remarkably, while the Bears had two portable heaters, they did not have portable seats on their sideline. It was also a day when Silky D was going to make history. He was going to become the first Chicago Bear receiver to rack up a pair of touchdowns in a playoff game and the first Chicago player to score two touchdowns in a postseason game since quarterback Bill Wade broke the plane on a pair of quarterback sneaks versus—how 'bout this?—the New York Giants back on December 29, 1963, some five weeks after the assassination of John Fitzgerald Kennedy, our thirty-fifth president.

The fans who shivered in Cubs Park during that '63 win by the Bears were still feeling the hangover, the emotional trauma, of what had gone down in Dallas with JFK. Yes, we were a very virginal nation, but there were already legions of skeptics who were convinced that alleged gunman Lee Harvey Oswald simply had not acted alone.

The backdrop for the '86 Bears-Giants showdown was significantly different. The Bears had cruised through the regular season 15 and 1. They were 9-point favorites over the Big Blue.

"Soldier Field is cold as hell in January," Dennis agrees, "especially for a kid from South Miami, Florida who just wasn't used to frigid temperatures. But it wasn't my first time. Forget about cold weather. Great players do. When you're cold you're consumed with thinking about how to get off the field. I recall before the season finale in 1983 versus Green Bay at Soldier Field, I suffered frostbite during the pre-game warm-up. Our wide outs coach Ted Plumb, my coaching angel, told me how to get back to normal. Ted had me hold my hands under warm water and then rub them down with Vaseline. Ted eventually had me hold on to heating pads before I put on a baseball gloves and then scuba gloves."

The cold was nothing compared to the pressure Chicago was putting on their Bears.

"Think about what was at stake. 1963 was a distant memory. The Bears were hosting a playoff game for the first time in what seemed like forever. I can still see Sean Landeta swinging and missing when he tried to punt about five yards from the Giants end zone. The wind just blew the ball away from Landeta so rapidly that he might have gotten one, maybe two, toes on the ball. Our Shaun Gayle scooped up the botched punt and could have gone on a two-hour walk into the end zone to give us an early 7-0 lead. But that's just a minor, somewhat comic, element to the narrative. The defense and Dennis McKinnon, yes, me, were going to make headlines.

I was in solid playing shape. The Bears had shut me down the last two weeks of the regular season to give my injured knee a chance to heal. So I had two weeks to mend, and since we had no real place to work out up at Halas Hall, the team traveled down to Suwanee, Georgia to prepare at the Atlanta Falcons training headquarters. So, add up the numbers, I had a full month to get ready for the Giants, and I really needed almost every day of that time. You can't shoot a knee like I got shot so damn many times that year and expect to heal in 48 hours."

I asked if he remembered the pre-game.

"Yep. Richard, Hampton, Mongo, Wilber, and Otis, the guts of the 46, were standing at midfield, staring and taunting Phil Simms, the Giants quarterback. They looked like a group of cheetahs on the Serengeti waiting to pounce on their prey. They're telling Simms, out of legendary Moorehead State, that he has no idea what's about to be unleashed on him. Three and half hours later Phil had been sacked six times—three and half of those by Richard. New York couldn't stop the sack man. Understand something about Dent and Dan Hampton. Hamp was a very good football player, but he became a ferocious Hall of Fame football player when Richard joined us in '83, and he began dealing with the bulk of the double-teams. Without the arrival of Richard, I don't think Dan's in the Hall."

We knew one thing for certain that afternoon versus the Giants. Two legendary announcers, Pat Summerall and John Madden, were going to be genuinely entertained. Think of Russell Crowe in the movie *Gladiator* saying, 'Are you not entertained' while Pat and John respond, 'Indeed, we are.'

I ask Silky if he and defensive back Elvis Patterson did any talking. "No," Dennis replies, "but this might surprise you. Elvis, unintentionally, left me face-first on the carpet after he tackled me on a reception. My lip was busted and I had an abrasion on my forehead right below my helmet. I was pissed the rest of the day. I knew I was going to be doing TV shots after the game and I had to look my best because, you know, there were gonna be girls watching. Don't mess up my face!

In a way, that explains why I never hung out with our defensive guys. They thought I was too cool, too flashy. I also didn't smoke or drink, and at the time, I was actually still a bit shy. I do remember one thing about that game, something I'll just never forget. We got graded after every game, and I was given a 97 after we looked at the Giants game on film on Monday. That really means I came up short on just one block."

Dennis obviously won the war against Elvis Patterson, but as I recall on both of his TD catches, Patterson played him tough. Both balls were what we now call 50-50 balls.

"That's almost always the case with a receiver," Dennis explains. "If you can't make a play, if you can't make the catch on the ball, you have to change gears. You have to make sure the d-back doesn't come up with a pick. You never hear TV commentators talk about that, but it's a big part of a wide receiver's responsibility."

I asked Dennis to break down the two catches he went to the house.

"On my first route we knew we had a free play since the Giants had jumped offside. I ran a simple go route and Elvis really did a solid job in coverage. I synced up with Jim and we scored from 23 yards out. People asked me what it felt like to score a touchdown in a playoff game on national TV. I told them to go back a year. I had gotten my feet wet 12 months earlier when I hooked up with Steve Fuller, Mac's caddy, for six against the Redskins at RFK. So, really, I just felt like I had been there before."

And the second TD?

"Before I get to that, I want to mention something. I got a game ball after that win over New York. It was one of, maybe, 14 or 15 game balls I picked up over the years. Some of those were for receiving, but most of them were for dirty work, the blocking, and special teams stuff I did. See if you see a common thread. I scored and picked up game balls versus the Redskins (one touchdown), the Giants (two touchdowns), and Philly (one touchdown) in the Fog Bowl in 1988. We obviously won all three of those games, which rates as another argument that I was terribly underutilized in the passing game."

Why was that?

"Politics. Fuckin' politics. Willie was the golden child, the first-round draft pick. I was the walk-on who sacrificed his body. That's the same Gault who froze me, his roommate, out of the *Super Bowl Shuffle*. I could be bitter about Willie and maybe I should be, but that's just not me. That's not how my mama raised me. I know in my heart what I accomplished on the football field."

I asked about the weather that day. Did it begin to get to him?

"No, if your hands and feet don't get cold you just don't get cold. Again, the lessons I learned from Ted Plumb, our receivers coach, about dealing with the cold were a tremendous asset to me. So, on the second score versus Patterson I ran another go route. Elvis was up in press (coverage) while the Giants' safety was not in his normal spot. Jim audibled and called out "Blue 72" and I got excited. I know it's a slant route and the linebacker on my side isn't gonna give Patterson any help because he's blitzing. I get help from Emery (Moorehead), our tight end, who ran a quick out to occupy another one of their linebackers. So, I did a quick stutter step with an in and out move to get Elvis off balance. Now, I use a swim move to get back inside. It was OVER at the line of scrimmage. Elvis never got a hand on me. Now, my job is to give Jim time to get off a three-step drop. Now, it becomes a battle of grit between two gifted athletes. Elvis, again, played me tough. His coverage wasn't soft. This was a battle of wills and on this play, I was just the better man. No, Elvis and I never talked. On the football field I didn't know anybody. I didn't want to know anybody."

I remind Dennis of the defense that day. Richard Dent, with three and half QB sacks, was virtually unstoppable…completely unblockable. The Giants couldn't stop the Sack Man. I thought his performance in that game was actually better than his effort in Super Bowl XX and, my god, he was chosen MVP in the main event.

"The world was introduced to Richard Dent in that win over the Giants," Dennis agrees. "That was Richard's coming out party. I'm sure Hampton wasn't crazy about Richard getting the pub. I'm sure you recall Mike Ditka chiding Dent by calling him Robert. How stupid was that? Richard made Ditka and the Bears eat their words in '85 because he led the league in sacks with 17. All Richard Dent ever did for Mike Ditka was make Mike money. There is no love lost here. Richard will tell you he blames Ditka for the Bears not winning back-to-back Super Bowls."

People misinterpreted Richard. He talked slowly and appeared from time to time to be off in his own world, half asleep. That was just how Richard was, but you can book this, Sack rates with Bruce Smith, the tough guy at Buffalo, when you talk about great pass rushers. Or let me rephrase, Bruce Smith rates with Dent on the Mount Rushmore of great pass rushers. That's damn good company.

### 

I asked Dennis if there was ever any finger pointing in the locker room during his years with the Bears.

"Guys may have talked under their breath and some guys got full of themselves. Think about comments Dan Hampton made about Jim McMahon. Hampton is still complaining that the Bears would have won another Super Bowl, maybe two more, if Jimmy Mac could have stayed on the field. We only won one Super Bowl, but it had a great deal to do with Jim McMahon. Hampton's comments are gutless."

I asked why he thought Hampton said things like that.

"He's a reformed alcoholic, and he's on my shortlist of guys who shouldn't have the yellow (Hall of Fame) jacket. You think Hampton ever mentioned that our offense led the league in rushing four consecutive years? Hampton has shown his true colors over the years with his hate for McMahon. You'll never hear Dan talk about us leading the league in time of possession in '85 or leading the NFL rushing from '83 through '86. Do you think Hampton ever offered praise to the brothers, guys I hung with like Mike Richardson, Leslie (Frazier), Double D (Dave Duerson), or Richard (Dent)? Hampton's in the Hall of Fame because Richard drew the double-teams. Hampton knows that. It's the truth."

# Chapter Five

The NFL would love to see spousal abuse disappear, along with CTE and claims from retired players who are financially tapped out and mentally broken from a game that's left them with the intellectual capacity of mayonnaise. I could give you 400 names of NFL players over the years who've taken a hand or fist to a female. Guys like Brandon Marshall, Santonio Holmes, Ray Rice, Dez Bryant, and Chad (Ochocinco) Johnson are names that come immediately to mind.

Ironically, the aforementioned are all African American. I asked Dennis if he believed there was a reason for that.

"A large majority of the men who do it have always been protected," Dennis points out. "They feel invincible, untouchable. Most of these guys have a screw loose. Most of the white players who do this stuff are protected by the league to make it look like a black issue. You know the old story…they're black people, that's just how they are. That is such bullshit. That's like the NFL saying it's concerned about player safety. Please, they're concerned about lawsuits. White fans don't want to talk about a white guy like Josh Brown, the former kicker for the Giants. The guy admitted he beat the hell out of his wife Molly. Brown admitted to being repulsive and treating his wife like a slave. So what did the Giants do? They signed him to a new contract worth four million bucks."

Eventually, when the heat got ramped up on Brown, the Giants released him. That leads us to John Mara, the third-generation owner of the Giants and a guy who we can assume came out of the womb with a silver spoon firmly lodged in his mouth. Mara waited far too long to oust Brown. He admitted he knew about the guy's abusive behavior towards his wife. That's in New York, the toughest media town in America. A black athlete would have been dumped on a pile of hot coals near Staten Island.

"Football players do have a tremendous degree of built-in aggression," Dennis admits, "controlled aggression. That's the code of playing hurt, playing without fear. It's a macho spirit based on a tolerance for pain that the average person can't begin to understand."

And players are exposed to a nearly unlimited supply of women who are interested.

"Yes," Dennis says, "and I know this will sound like preaching, but you can't be tempted by the devil. Women can be satanic to a kid trying to make a football team. It's hard to think about women when you're a walk-on trying to make the team. You know the overhead camera, the eye in the sky, followed all of our moves, captured every mistake. It didn't take any prisoners."

Of course, spousal abuse is something very different.

"It's a very sad and tragic state of affairs that fans see spousal abuse as just a black problem," Dennis says again. "Whites are comfortable believing it's a product of the black environment. Again, that's just bullshit. Combine that with the fact that fans and people who don't follow football are jealous of the money players make. Now, let's throw in interracial dating and marriage. Listen to me, and I mean this, a white woman is the black player's kryptonite. She knows how to play the game. White girls have memorized the playbook on landing black athletes. They don't know, the public doesn't have a clue, that black players are raised to believe that their mothers are queens. It's very sad, very troubling. When you raise a hand to a woman, a person so physically inferior, you're raising your hand directly to your mother. When Donald Trump said to guys like Colin Kaepernick that they were sons of bitches that should get off their knees, all players with a mom should have kneeled."

I asked Silky to explain something to this aging white guy who can't dance. After Mike Tyson did three and a half years in the joint in Indiana for the sexual assault of Desiree Washington, I attended his initial comeback fight in Las Vegas versus Peter McNeeley, a tomato can from Boston. Don King, Tyson's front man, was no dummy. He knew Mike was rusty and maybe a little disinterested, so he wasn't going to put him in the ring against a guy who could actually bust a grape.

For the record, 10 seconds into the fight, McNeeley was already on his back. The bout ended 89 seconds into the first round by disqualification. McNeeley wasn't just frightened, he was unequivocally afraid to walk out of the dressing room. Now, hear me out, before the bout, Tyson emerged, black trunks, black boots, no socks—his traditional gear—to a massive ovation, especially from black women. I have to admit the response from females of color shocked me.

"Black women were saying we know Mike was set up like so many other black men have been set up," Dennis explains. "There was no real evidence, no eyewitnesses. Just two adults in the Canterbury Hotel in Indianapolis. Those girls were saying, we know Mike was a fall guy. We knew he never had a chance in court. They understand the word redemption."

For the record, Lester Munson, the former legal expert at *Sports Illustrated*, a journalistically brilliant man, told me the defense provided for Mike by Vincent Fuller brought new meaning to the word "pathetic."

Another domestic abuse case was in the news and became a topic of discussion. Urban Meyer resigned, leaving the school with an unblemished 7 and 0 record versus Michigan. I asked Silk how Urban should be remembered.

"Meyer is a great coach but a terrible, lying ass of a human being. He won with all the programs he guided, but there was always the hint of scandal. His handling of domestic abuse with his assistant coach was absolutely disgraceful. Domestic abuse in this country is in full color. Meyer never took time to notice. I guess the phrase 'leader of men' doesn't transfer over to how assistant coaches treat women."

After the 2018 season the Bears briefly made noises about possibly signing a known domestic abuser, Kareem Hunt.

"I guess a guy who dares to kneel in peaceful protest (Colin Kaepernick) can't get a job," Dennis points out, "but hitting a player, belting a woman, is the lesser of two supposed evils. Females who support the NFL should stand up and take notice."

Before we go diving off the Olympic high board, just keep one thought front and center—how would have 96-year-old Virginia McCaskey reacted to the Bears adding Hunt to the roster? The NFL's grand old gal, a pillar of dignity, was born in 1923, roughly two years before the Bears signed a guy named Red Grange. She is also the matriarch who thought sideline cheerleaders were just a bit too racy, so shortly after the Bears won the Super Bowl, she bopped the Honey Bears.

Mrs. McCaskey signing off on Kareem Hunt? I'd make that 300 to 1. (Hunt would eventually sign with the Cleveland Browns, the most active club in the 2019 free agent circuit with one drawback. He will sit out the first eight games of the new season due to violations of the league conduct policy. Naturally, Hunt's miscue was decking a woman.)

"Why would the Bears talk about or consider bringing in Hunt?" Dennis asks. "I guess it validates that winning is far more important than anything else on your moral compass. I have enormous respect for Mrs. McCaskey. I felt terrible for her when her husband Ed passed away back in 2003. Ed was great guy to be around. To many of us who played back in the 80s, she is like the Rose Bowl is to college kids today—the granddaddy or grand mama of them all.

Put it this way, to get to the queen you have to go through the thickets of mud, you almost have to go through hell. In the case of the Bears, that means Hunt would have had to meet with Ryan Pace and Matt Nagy—that's the easy part. Nagy had stars in his eyes over Kareem, he coached the kid at K.C. Club president Ted Phillips and, of course, George McCaskey would also have to be addressed before he could earn his ticket to visit with Mrs. McCaskey. I don't believe George would have ever signed off on Hunt because in his eyes I think he would feel he would be showing disrespect to his mother."

TMZ got its hands on a video clearly showing Hunt trying to kick and punch the hell out of a woman in a Cleveland elevator on shortly after 3:00 a.m. on February 10, 2018. The incident is a vivid reminder of ex-Baltimore Raven, Ray Rice, flying off the handle in 2014 when he cold-cocked his fiancée in—good morning!—a hotel elevator.

"The NFL is a place where domestic violence and abuse had been swept under the rug for decades," Dennis says. "The Ray Rice mess changed the situation. The Rice video doesn't lie. Things had to change since a vast number of females are NFL fans and plenty of those females are moms. I had a teammate with the Bears back in the 80s, a guy still very prominent in Chicago, who was slugging his wife. The pathetic thing about what was going on was this 6'3" hunk of muscle bragged about raising a hand to his wife, or maybe at that time it was his ex-wife."

My gut reaction? Mrs. McCaskey would reach new levels of anger if Pace approached her about adding someone like Hunt.

###

With the subject of his mother broached again, I asked Dennis about how much he helped her financially after he joined the Bears.

"I really wish I could have given the world to Mama," he says. "Today's athletes who make it to the professional level in any sport almost always use their bonus money to buy their mama a new home or a car. Note, I didn't say parents, I said MOTHERS because with so many black athletes it's just the mothers who are raising them, protecting them, and trying to steer them on the right course. I never got the big bonus, I got peanuts, so the best thing I could do to honor Mama was to graduate from Florida State. I know that meant far more to her than anything I did on a football field. I was the first kid in our family to get a college degree. I couldn't let Mama down. With what money I did have, I paid her bills and bought her a Cadillac. It was me showing respect and appreciation for the way she raised me. That never changed.

I know how much my degree meant to Mama. That was the realization of a dream for her when I got that diploma. Believe me, everybody in town knew Mrs. McKinnon. She really had her own fan club. She was a woman, a devout Baptist, who treated people with grace and dignity. She loved standing in the kitchen singing the sounds of people like Albertina Walker, Shirley Caesar, Gladys Knight along with James Cleveland and Sam Cooke. Mama could really sing. Yes, I went to church every Sunday. No, she never spanked or whipped me. Her words, her love, carried far more passion."

I wondered if Dennis had ever considered another career.

"I studied criminology at FSU," he said. "I really thought I might become an attorney or go into some form of law enforcement."

I asked if he ever considered modeling.

"It might have worked for me, but it wasn't what I wanted. You know the way I dressed, always kept my hair perfect, and my nails looking good, some people thought I was gay. It didn't take me long to bust that illusion."

Dennis smiled his electric, made-for-TV smile.

# Chapter Six

Back in 1985 Chicago wasn't the "City with the Big Shoulders," it was a political reality series. Harold Washington was in office as the city's first black mayor. He had 21 aldermen, 16 blacks and five white guys who sided with him versus the so-called Vrdolyak 29. The Vrdolyak team, led by Alderman "Fast Eddie" Vrdolyak, who was always an inch away from getting busted for some kind of political corruption, consisted of 28 whites and one Hispanic. There wasn't a helluva lot the city council did to improve Chicago during this time, but the "Council Wars" made for great theater. Legendary columnist Mike Royko, a laconic, bone-breaking, yet passionate scribe, had a field day writing about the nonsense at City Hall. But despite the drama on the political scene, the city united around their boys in blue and orange. Somehow, they eclipsed the drama taking place at City Hall.

The leader of the band was Mike Ditka.

"You know what I'll always remember about Mike Ditka?" Dennis says. "At a Monday morning film session after a ballgame, Mike stopped the film, did a rewind, ran the play again and told our guys, 'If everybody blocked like McKinnon, we'd never lose.' You can't quantify what that means to a guy, especially a player who always sold out, never worried about his body."

I asked if Ditka ever intimidated any of the guys. "No, not really," Dennis replies. "We all thought of ourselves as alpha males, and I think Ditka knew that. It's interesting that when a guy made a mistake Ditka would yell at his position coach—not at the player. When Walter made a mistake, Mike would carve up Johnny Roland (running backs coach). When Otis messed up, Mike would go after

Dave McGinnis (linebackers coach). If I screwed up, Ted Plumb (wide receiver coach) would get a mouthful. Our title club knew it didn't need Ditka. Yes, Mike was a great motivator, but most of his bravado was about impressing the media. Mike Ditka saw my edge early in my first training camp. Even before we played our first exhibition, Ditka was telling people I was going to make the ball club."

So what happened with Mike and the Bears?

"Ditka's bullying worked for really a long time," Dennis says. "He had terrific players, but those players responded for him and produced. Eventually, guys got sick of his act and gave up on him. Ditka took too much credit away from the guys who made him rich. You know, why can't Ditka, who is worth a fortune, give a broken-down 'Fridge' Perry $3,000 a month? We all know that Ditka made a bundle off the Fridge. When Ditka was the Alpha Dog, his players responded. Eventually the alpha dog edge wore thin. People forget the train wreck Mike was during his three years in New Orleans after he left the Bears. Mike went 15 and 33. Maybe the game had passed him by.

Look at Jon Gruden with the Raiders, still getting praise for the Super Bowl he won with Tampa and Tony Dungy's players back in 2002. When he made the move to Oakland, he'd been away from the sidelines for almost a decade."

I asked Dennis about Buddy Ryan, the Bears' legendary defensive coordinator.

"You know, Buddy didn't have much use for the brothers. He put (Dan) Hampton, Steve McMichael and Gary Fencik up on a pedestal, but he really didn't seem to like the brothers. Wilber Marshall was the best run stopper, cover linebacker of my era. He deserves to be placed on the same plane with Derrick Brooks. Wilber was quiet unless he knew you. He also played angry, hostile. I think some of Wilber's rage was fueled by how Buddy treated him. Ryan saw his defensive players as mindless mannequins, but his guys did like Buddy because he was upfront and honest to a fault. I just wish Buddy had offered some praise to the brothers."

It was a different era.

"Ryan couldn't get away with his crap today," Dennis agrees. "Players have money we never dreamed of seeing. A guy Buddy would call out could tell Ryan, I've got 30 million in guaranteed money, what have you got? Let's be honest about Buddy. What did he (joined Bears in 1978) really accomplish with the Bears' defense before the class of '83 arrived, followed by Wilber Marshall in '84? The answer is really not much. Buddy did do one thing, he protected his pets. Gary Fencik was a tremendous tackler and a solid blitz guy, but he was very weak in coverage. Buddy had to set our defense to make sure Gary wasn't left on an island."

Speaking of tacklers, I told Dennis that Wilber Marshall wasn't the greatest fundamental guy I've ever seen tackle, but I have never seen anybody hit with greater ferocity, including Dick Butkus—nobody, case closed. McKinnon agreed.

"(Mike) Singletary belongs in the Hall of Fame, but NOT when Wilber Marshall isn't anywhere near the Shrine in Canton, Ohio. Wilber was the superior player. Singletary played the media. Wilber didn't care about the press. This is fact: the white media saw Singletary as a black man who was white. That was significant in terms of Mike's popularity. How tough was Wilber? Mountains like Dan Hampton were intimidated by Wilber. You know Buddy Ryan saw Singletary as his go-to guy, his Judas who would play the role of company man with Buddy. When you were around Singletary and, this is real, Gary Fencik, you had to watch what you said because those guys were going right back to management. Singletary would tell Buddy what he thought Buddy wanted to hear."

We'll get into the race issue more deeply in a future chapter, but we can't go on before Dennis lays this little nugget on me about the 1985 Bears.

"The black guys used to joke with the white guys about speed. We'd tell back-up linebackers like Ron Rivera and Jim Morrissey that if they picked up a loose ball, they should pitch it to a brother."

### 

The subject turns to college football, and Dennis also has some strong opinions on that subject. Silky had just gotten back from the Big 10 title game in Indianapolis where Urban Meyer, a guy you can learn to dislike quicker than you can say "speeding ticket," took time to get the Ohio State motor running but wound up watching his kids overwhelm Northwestern 45-24. I suggest to Dennis that in a year or two, Fitz should vacate his cozy lair in Evanston to coach a school where he can play for a national title. Fitz is a hot name. Any number of football factories would love to have him. I mention that to Dennis, and Silk thinks I need to be locked up and given immediate mental help.

"He'll never do it and really, why should he?" Dennis says. "He doesn't have to be an alpha dog at Northwestern, he's not going to have his name blown up on Twitter if he loses to Michigan or Penn State. He's in the cozy Big 10 West, not exactly a division on overload with great football teams. He's not making Nick Saban-type cash ($11,000,000 a year), but he's making great money and the school probably pays for his house. All Fitz has to do is win seven games and go to a second- or third-tier bowl game. He's under no pressure to fill the ballpark. The alumni don't expect Pat to beat the powerhouses. I'd love to play for Fitz. He gets everything out of his players and he's not a bully. He's not gonna make a player look stupid. In other words, he's not like Nick Saban."

Silk is not a Saban fan.

"Saban has the easiest job in college football. Nobody remembers that he went 15-17 in two lackluster years as head coach of the Dolphins. Saban knows why he's winning big at Alabama. The brothers have embraced his culture, which tells you Nick can't coach men—pro football players—but he can bully kids."

I asked Silky who was more insufferable, Saban or Meyer?

"Urban Meyer's conduct over the last decade, Florida, the Buckeyes, has been intolerable. He's a disgrace to college football. I just hated the way Gus Johnson, the Fox football announcer, just gushed about Urban during Ohio State's win over (Jim) Harbaugh and Michigan. Johnson was pathetic. Meyer actually got away with telling people he wasn't aware of his wide receivers coach, Zach Smith, abusing his wife on numerous occasions. Urban's wife knew, but Urban was too busy preparing for his big games with Tulane and Rutgers to have any clue about the Smith guy. Gus Johnson chose to overlook that little episode. Wives talk. It's how they are. You know Meyer knew his assistant was guilty as hell, but Johnson decided his role in life was to be Urban's P.R. man. Gus apparently didn't know that Ohio State was tone deaf to the situation with Urban. Johnson is broadcasting disgrace. The school had an obligation to fire Meyer on the spot, immediately. Instead, he wound up with a three-game—paid—suspension as the Buckeyes brass did its own form of Buckeye Nation damage control."

Does that situation remind Dennis of anyone else?

"It does bear some resemblance to Joe Paterno spending years looking the other way while Jerry Sandusky was abusing young kids. Paterno knew what Sandusky was doing. He made no effort to stop what the guy was doing. Nobody ever questioned Joe because in Happy Valley he knew the rules didn't apply to him. Sometimes you have to wonder who controls the moral compass. Look at how much money the

Catholic church has spent to cover up for priests who were abusing kids. How many times did the church just have a guilty priest switch parishes only to see the same man of the cloth commit another crime against a young and frightened kid? Here again, like Paterno, when you wear the cloth you can't be questioned. Those who were guilty shouldn't walk."

I broach the subject of former Bears coach Lovie Smith, currently holding down the fort in Champaign-Urbana.

"I guarantee you the players have no respect for Lovie," Dennis says. "Look, Illinois made what it thought was a safe play with Smith. They hired a former NFL coach. The school thought it was creating an earthquake of excitement. It was rolling 7s. Instead, the hire came up snake eyes. It's an embarrassment to all involved in Lovie's hiring. You know Northwestern is like watching paint dry, but they are winning. A lot of that is about Fitz (Coach Pat Fitzgerald). I know Northwestern has to have a rival school travel big to fill its ballpark, but kids do want to play football for the Cats. On the other hand, what kid is just dying to play at Illinois? Sadly, it's become a prison sentence."

So help me, Bob Zuppke (Google him up, he's worth it), Illinois A.D. Josh Whitman, with absolutely no fanfare whatsoever, announced on the school website that he was extending Smith's contract two more years. Wins-losses? Who cares? Alumni apathy? Who cares? A student body that hates Illinois football? Who cares?

When I see Lovie, I see a Greek tragedy. Whitman sees Lovie and apparently sees Bear Bryant or Knute Rockne. He also sees Lovie with so much guaranteed money on his original contract that Whitman just can't dump him, so he may as well give Smith time to continue his rebuild.

"This is the dumbest, stupidest single coaching move I can ever recall," Dennis says, piling on. "Illinois football is now non-existent. The school has told all six or seven people left in its fan base that it doesn't give a damn about winning. Kids live and die on social media. They know how miserable Illinois is. If an 18-year-old kid is driving downstate and sees a sign saying the Illinois campus is two miles ahead, he only has one option—keep on driving. Illinois will completely fail what's left of its fan base and the State of Illinois if it doesn't fire Lovie Smith. I don't care what the buyout is."

I asked Dennis about the combine—the annual NFL-Indianapolis meat market.

"The combine is a waste of time," he opines. "If guys can't run a 4.32 in the 40-yard dash or he's not 6'3', but just 6'1", they're already in an uphill battle. The combine is about running, jumping, and throwing against air. Think about that—air is your opponent. What does that really tell you about a guy's versatility? The Wonderlic test to measure a guy's I.Q. or whatever is bullshit. If a guy can play, you're going to draft him. If he completely fails the Wonderlic? Didn't they used to have a question that read, 'If you were a tree, what kind of tree would you be?' If I took the test I'd say one that doesn't have hanging fruit."

For the benefit of the house, the legendary Wonderlic was first used by Tom Landry back in the 60s when he was coaching the Dallas Cowboys. For history buffs, Eldon F. Wonderlic, a graduate student at Northwestern University, is credited with creating the beloved test of one's cerebral gifts or lack thereof.

"The player interviews are basically useless," Dennis adds. "Agents coach their players on what teams want to hear. Guys can look like total dummies, but if they can play, or if clubs at least think they can play, they can still make 20 million a year no matter how high they jump or how many questions they flub on the Wonderlic."

# Chapter Seven

318-pound white 0-linemen would never have been regulars on "Soul Train" when the Train master, husky-voiced Don Cornelius, with lapels and ties as wide as riverboats, was hosting "The Train." I ask Dennis, 'Is Matt Nagy running his postgame disco, a play on Joe Maddon's post dance parties with the Cubs, to tell his black players, 'I'm with you. You can trust me because I understand what your life is all about'?

"No," Dennis says. "I just think it's part of where our society is culturally. Nagy does want to make his black players feel comfortable. Do the math, how many players on his roster or any NFL roster are African Americans? Today's athletes of color are very sensitive about everything. They should be. Look at how the league ostracized and blackballed Colin Kaepernick. He's been gone since 2016 while the league has white quarterbacks who aren't worth a damn scattered all over the league. You know what really never died? The notion that blacks can't play quarterback. Morons think you can play with a black quarterback, but you can't win with a black quarterback. People who think like that are idiots, mental degenerates."

Is racism still alive and well in the NFL?

"I do my best not to look at everything in black and white terms," Dennis answers. "Unfortunately, the world does, or most of it. I admire rap/hip hop artists like Rihanna and Cardi B for refusing to perform at the Super Bowl. They were showing solidarity with Colin. These kids were giving up massive, once-in-a-lifetime shots of exposure. There's no money paid to the performers for the title game because the NFL figures it's doing the artists it selects a big favor. By the way, Maroon

Five wasn't the league's choice to perform at the Super Bowl. Atlanta as the host city made the choice to offer up the gig to Maroon."

I ask Dennis, if Kaepernick had been his teammate, would he have kneeled with him? Would Walter have kneeled with him?

"Yes, Walter and I would have both kneeled with him in protest of police brutality and the continued mistreatment of blacks as a race. I really believe our entire ball club would have been united with Colin, locked arm in arm, to show support for what he was protesting. How much police brutality do blacks have to absorb? I know it's 2019, but in many regards the slave mentality is still very much part of our culture. In many regards, things aren't much different than they were back in '64 before Lyndon Johnson passed civil rights legislation. Look at how Dan Gilbert, the Cavs owner, treated LeBron James when he left the club to move to Miami. Gilbert made it very clear that he thought LBJ was his slave. His words, his language and tone of voice, told people in his words, I OWN LeBron."

Is it also that way in the NFL?

"Of course," Dennis says. "I understand why players kneel. I wish athletes would do it year around and not just on Sundays in the fall. No matter what the black athletes do, they won't please everybody. America has been good but never great for African Americans. Our country was built on bigotry and lies. History tells us that there are so many veterans, people I know personally in some cases, and first responders who I truly offer respect and admiration. My brother served with honor for 30 years in the Army. However, if you take the time to visit V.A. hospitals and you see how our veterans have been treated miserably or how warped with depression they are, so many who came back from Nam or Iraq who have been disrespected, it makes one raise the American flag with a lesser degree of enthusiasm."

Is there hypocrisy there—among kneeling critics?

"Put it this way," Dennis says. "I make it a point to go to a lot of sporting events. When you hear the national anthem playing, I ask people to stop for a moment and look at how many people haven't removed their hats or placed a hand on their heart. They're too busy texting. If a man's in his late 60s or 70s and he did two or maybe three tours in Vietnam, how is he supposed to feel? Do we ever think about the trauma he's endured, trauma that will never go away?"

"I've said this before and I'll say it again," Dennis continues. "The biggest threat to white society is a black man with verbal skills, especially an educated black man with verbal skills who dares to speak the truth. I know my history. I know what black folks have gone through over the past 150 years. Nobody has to tell me about Martin Luther King, Rosa Parks, Medgar Evers, or Emmitt Till."

I ask if he feels sorry for Colin.

"Yes, I do feel sorry for Colin," Dennis replies. "Do you notice that the mainstream media doesn't talk about the record money Nike did with its #Justdoit ad campaign with Colin? Does anybody remember that Kaepernick led the 49ers to a Super Bowl when Jim Harbaugh was running the show with the 49ers? In '85, things were much different for NFL players. We had to work our asses off to make a living. We had to fight to get an extra pair of socks. I'm not kidding. Our unity was rock solid."

Even with a superstar like Walter Payton?

"He was the face of the NFL in the 80s. What kind of pressure would the league have felt if Walter had been kneeling side by side with Colin Kaepernick? I don't think the league would have known what to do. How would the NFL take on Sweetness? The answer is they couldn't. The NFL would have been hamstrung. I wish today's players really understood what Walter meant to the game. Do they know that in '87 when we went on strike—and forced free agency—that

Walter dipped into his own pocket to help teammates pay bills when we weren't getting game checks? That's a true story. Do they comprehend the fact that the Walter Payton NFL Man of the Year award is the highest individual honor the league has to offer? Yet, this has to be brought to the table. Again, the NFL good old boys club denied Walter the right to purchase the old St. Louis Rams franchise. I'll let our readers draw their own conclusions."

Will Kaepernick ever be back?

"Colin Kaepernick never had a chance against the most powerful league for the obvious reason: he's not white. He's biracial, so in the eyes of the league and the ticket-buying public, he's black. Look at the oval office. Look at how President Obama was treated in comparison to President Bush or President Trump. Look at the league. The owners are all white. If they weren't, there would be no need for the Rooney Rule. Television is supported by the privileged, while the vast majority of the league's players are of color—black. Blacks are the reason why the public pays ungodly prices to buy tickets and merchandise with the team's logo."

But the players get a fairer share of the total than they used to, right?

"Let's face it, the league is full of overpaid players regardless of color. That also applies to head coaches. You can spin it any way you want. This is fact. The black coach may have a solid record on the college or NFL record, but he is only going to get the mandatory interview— blacks just don't get the jobs. Take it or leave it, but it's fact."

Silk and I begin to munch on cheeseburgers as the conversation does a 180 and moves to Tiger Woods and Serena Williams. I tell Dennis it'll be murder1 if Woods isn't chosen 2018 comeback athlete of the year.

"You know why I admire Tiger and Serena so much? They climbed hills they weren't supposed to climb. For example, Serena grew up in Compton—she's not supposed to excel at a country club sport. Let's face it, tennis and golf are white people's games. In this country sports are supposed to be sacred with no room for politics or racism, but we both know that's not the case. Guys like Dustin Johnson and Justin Thomas owe a big share of their earnings to Tiger. Who watches golf to see Thomas and Johnson? The answer is nobody. They're like watching paint dry."

What makes Tiger so special?

"What Tiger did this year was phenomenal. He was ranked 1,119th by the PGA at the end of 2017. Now think about this—when he shut down in '18, he was ranked 13th. Who does that? Look at what Tiger's had to deal with. Critics, broadcasters, writers who can't hide the fact that they don't want Tiger on the same pedestal with Jack Nicklaus or Arnold Palmer. Those people are telling you that a brother shouldn't be the best. Look at the break-up between Tiger and his ex-wife Elin Nordgren. Tiger's black. Elin's white. If Elin had been black, the story would have been in one ear and out the other. Woods' fall from grace was all about him being with a white woman other than his wife. Even with some blacks, there is an issue when it comes to interracial dating or marriage."

I wasn't expecting such passion on this subject, but Silky wasn't done.

"Go back in history. The constitution was written by racists. Black athletes are still looked upon as entertainment. Tiger and Serena know this: as great as they are, they are not the boss. The boss is the guy whose name is on the bottom of the check. Blacks learn it doesn't matter how intellectual you are. There are people who look at Michelle Obama and say, yes, you're brilliant, but you're still black. So there are reasons why blacks are angry. Muhammad Ali was elegant and incredibly verbal. The power of his voice frightened white people. When Ali made the conversion to Islam, he became a threat to people."

But the ratings numbers don't lie. Tiger and Serena are big draws.

"Think about how often you see Tiger almost shot-for-shot on Saturday and Sunday when he's six strokes back. The public can't get enough of him. Tiger relearned something this year. Forget about the galleries that mob you. He learned how to win for himself."

### 

Adrian Peterson is back in the headlines. Sadly, this remarkably gifted running back, who has won enough hardware to fill up seven trophy cases, has been called out for admitting that he has punished his kids by spanking them with a belt, making them do squats, and taking away their electronic games. Go back to 2014. The NFL suspended Peterson, then the 5-star marquee running back for the Minnesota Vikings—and perhaps the most attractive ball carrier in the NFL—for harshly punishing his then-four-year-old son. The penalty imposed by the league cost A.P. over four million dollars in salary and effectively negated his contract with the Viks.

Dennis has some advice for Peterson.

"Adrian, my brother, protect your name, your brand. The NFL is run by white people who don't understand the black culture for punishing children. The fucking league doesn't really care what you do with your son or any of your kids, they just want to preserve the precious red, white, and blue NFL logo. But, Adrian, hear me out. Why talk about it? Why tell some reporter fishing for a story, an angle, about your home life? He wasn't asking you about a ballgame or about a rival defense. He was trying to get you to spill.

A.P. was the only reason Vikings fans had to show up. He was the best running back in the league. The league suspension was supported by Ziggy Wilf, the Vikings owner, who I'm sure was getting pressure from TV and radio sponsors. Minnesota refused to give Adrian a long-term deal in 2015, but the club turns around and gives a fully guaranteed three-year, 84-million-dollar deal to Kirk "Fucking" Cousins, a guy who's never won a playoff game. He's never won a playoff game!"

He's not the only one.

"I know. Hell, look at Ford Field in Detroit. The Lions gave Matt Stafford a 135-million-dollar deal with 60.5 million locked in—guaranteed. The Bears are lucky. They get to play these losers four times a year. If Cousins and Stafford left the NFL today, how would they be remembered? The answer is they wouldn't be remembered. They have carved no niche."

### 

Before we leave the subject of race, I ask Dennis about the big news of 2018 in Chicago: the cop Jason Van Dyke, who was sentenced to prison for killing Laquan McDonald. As we spoke in February of 2019, the news came out about the beating several inmates at the Danbury Corrections Center in Connecticut administered to the former cop. I ask Dennis if he has any sympathy at all for Van Dyke.

"I have no pity for Jason Van Dyke," Silk says. "His worst days are still down the road."

Silky and I look at a visual that depicts both Rosa Parks and Colin Kaepernick riding in the back of a bus with deeply forlorn expressions. Dennis also tells me with thorough conviction that he would have walked across the infamous Edmund Pettus Bridge in Selma, Alabama back in the early 60s where Dr. Martin Luther King and some 600 followers were met by racist cops waving billy clubs and hurling tear gas, along with raging dogs, in a display of hatred that shocked people around the world. The bridge was named after a general from the Civil War era back in the 1860s. That figures.

"Too many cops look at black people as target practice," Dennis says.

I was curious enough about Van Dyke getting KO'd to place a call to longtime friend, and former ESPN legal sports expert, Lester Munson. Lester has been a go-to guy for me on sports and the law since the Mike Tyson trial back in the early 90s.

"Several things about the Van Dyke beating shocked me," Lester tells me. "One, why was he moved from a state prison in Rock Island to a federal lock-up in Connecticut. I'm just in disbelief that he was placed in the general population. Really, why does he go from a state prison in Rock Island to a federal penitentiary in Connecticut? It leads me to this conclusion. Van Dyke was set up by someone or a group of people in the federal system. I'm not big on conspiracy theories, but I genuinely believe that someone at Danbury or with close ties to Danbury arranged to have Van Dyke set up to be attacked. The story just doesn't add up. I believe the Van Dyke beating was not a crime of opportunity but a crime of conspiracy."

Dennis didn't disagree but offered this as an additional thought.

"Blacks are set up to get beaten in prison every day, but you never hear a word about it. Nobody cares. The guys inside hate wife beaters, snitches, child molesters, and cops. The beating Van Dyke allegedly endured was a couple of inmates telling him you didn't get a real sentence in court, so we'll give you your sentence in here. Do you think the guys inside at Danbury didn't know about Van Dyke and what he did to Laquan?"

Tiffany Van Dyke, the wife of former officer Jason Van Dyke, says she's demanding that Governor Pritzker and Illinois State Attorney General Kwame Raoul provide answers on what took place with her husband. Meanwhile, Tammy Wendt, one of Van Dyke's attorneys, said her client was "a lamb led to slaughter."

"Again, I have no pity for Van Dyke," Dennis says. "It made my day when I heard he got mugged inside. That's small potatoes for committing murder. I'm also sick of Van Dyke's wife talking about how concerned she is about her old man. Shut up! Your old man killed a guy. It still amazes me that a guy who shot Laquan McDonald 16 times is doing just six years in prison. You know, if I can stand beside you in darkness, we can be brothers, yet racism sometimes has a way of finding its path to the front seat. Van Dyke is a symbol of privilege. He is a graphic example of the police brutality that blacks endure every day. It's just so appalling. The Laquan McDonald sentencing showed us a lot. For one, it showed me that Black History Month is February, the shortest month of the year."

I bring the subject back to a discussion of the NFL and wonder aloud, where the NFL will be in 10 years? Will there be an NFL in 10 years? The answer, of course, is yes. The TV money isn't going anywhere.

"Obviously, the league will have a new commissioner," Dennis says. "That's a blessing since Roger Goodell is just a P.R. man. Goodell doesn't have the passion for the game, or the league, that a Pete Rozelle or Paul Tagliabue brought to our sport. In some respects, Goodell reminds me of Mike Ditka. Goodell milks the NFL, while Ditka has spent 35 years milking the success of the '85 Bears."

What will change with a new commissioner?

"Pension money will increase. It has to. My pension is about three thousand dollars a month, a laughable number in comparison to Major League Baseball, the NBA, and the NHL."

Several hours after Silky and I talked, a bombshell of a story broke. Ex-49ers quarterback Colin Kaepernick reached a settlement with the NFL in his collusion case against the league. Kaepernick had claimed, with no small degree of justification, that the league had blackballed him in 2017 and '18 for kneeling during national anthems before games in 2016. Colin's former San Francisco teammate Eric Reid was also part of the suit.

My first reaction was simple: The NFL really had no choice but to reach accord and basically give in to Kaepernick. The NFL doesn't like to lose, but worse than that, it hates to disclose anything, and gosh only knows how many texts and emails were exchanged by the league and club owners regarding Kaepernick. But the key is nondisclosure. The NFL will never admit it, but the league could have suffered significant damages if "private info" had gone public. Colin's NIKE ad campaign was a grandiose success, and now he has beaten the NFL. It amazes me to see just how many people are finally hopping on the Kaepernick bandwagon.

"The NFL has always been a collection of bullies," Dennis says. "Now, with Colin vindicated, people are anxious to hop on his bandwagon. So naturally a large part of our society wants a slice of that vindication to call its own. The league basically paid Colin to go away."

# Chapter Eight

I have never met Marc Paskow, an incredibly vibrant octogenarian, who was Dennis's football coach at South Miami Senior High School. Yet Marc, who also mentored prep wrestlers and weight lifters, feels like an extended family member. His personality brings new meaning to the word "charming."

"Marc and I are living proof that blacks and Jews can get along with each other," Dennis points out. "To think otherwise is bullshit. I love Marc. We've had a bond that's lasted 40 years. I'll call him twice a week during the football season and usually three times a week during the offseason. I'm going to Miami next week for nine days, and my first two days will be spent with Marc."

This next yarn is just one for the book. We begin with Dennis and his old coach watching Marc's daughter play a high school soccer game.

"Dennis was burned up about the officiating," his old coach says. "He was on the referee all night. Finally, the ref walks right past Dennis over to me and hands me a yellow card or some kind of penalty. You know Dennis. If he sees something he doesn't like, he's going to speak up."

"The ref walked 10 yards past me," Dennis adds, "and got in Marc's face. Coach said, 'Wait a minute, can't you see the difference between Dennis and me?'"

Dennis explains the depth of his relationship with Marc and his family.

"I just love Marc's daughters. I attended both of their Bat Mitzvahs. I was given a yarmulke and wore it with pride. I'm so proud of both of Coach's daughters and the fact that they have always called me Uncle

Dennis. You know Marc is a relationship guy. He may be tiny, but he carries himself with a big stick. I learned one heck of a lot of football just by talking with him. You know my dad didn't offer me any help that got me to the NFL. He never bothered to attend one of my games at Florida State. My dad's culture was simple, as long as I was under his thumb things were okay. He never wanted to ride the bus with me, but he didn't hesitate to jump on the bus as my reputation grew."

Silk takes a bite out of his arugula salad and then keeps on firing.

"I've got one more soccer moment I want you to hear about. Marc and I were watching the game we're discussing. His daughter Amy is getting crowded by other girls, and the ref has swallowed his whistle. Again, I'm yelling like crazy as the ref walks right by me and glares at Marc. I remember Marc saying, 'I'm 5'7", it wasn't me, it was him.' Later Amy had the ball stolen from her and the rival team went on to score a goal that turned out to be the game winner. Amy was crying like she was hurt. I told Marc she's not hurt, she's just embarrassed. I told her to get up, suck it up, and reminded her there's no crying in soccer."

Marc's brain never slips from fifth gear down to third. He is a rapid-fire string of opinions and observations. It's obvious he has great respect for Dennis. During one gab session, he got on Michael Irvin's case.

"I don't get why punk asses like Michael Irvin get TV time and Dennis, who's so well-spoken, doesn't. What's with that?" he asks.

Dennis has an answer.

"Being a Dallas Cowboy gives you a lot of free room. Michael's rejoicing because he's not in jail. Every day he's on the street, it's a win."

What about Irvin's football skills?

"People often refer to Michael Irvin as the greatest possession receiver in NFL history," Dennis says. "That's incorrect. Michael wasn't a possession receiver. Guys like Steve Largent are possession receivers. But Michael Irvin is one of the greatest physical specimens in football history. He had tremendous hands, and I know from spending time with him when I was in Dallas in 1990 that he was a tireless worker. Hear me out…Michael Irvin worked every bit as hard in practice as Walter Payton did with our club. He also had great leadership qualities. You know there was never any animosity or friction between Michael and Emmitt Smith. They were very close. Two big stars, but very close, with strong mutual respect. Emmitt knew he had a gift with Michael's presence. Teams couldn't load eight or nine guys in the box with Irvin on the field. As a pass catcher, I can't recall anybody who ran the out route with greater authority than Michael."

I think I spot a twinkle in Dennis's eye. His next comment lets me know I'm not seeing things.

"You know Michael is married to one of my former girlfriends," he says, "a lady named Sandy Harrell. We dated during the late 1980s. I'm happy for the two of them. I'm not a jealous man."

I bring the subject back to Dennis's high school days. It's not every day you have a chance to speak to someone who was there for Dennis's football birth.

"I didn't encourage Dennis to attend Florida State," coach Marc says. "In fact, when Bobby Bowden showed up at our school for a visit, the first thing I said to him was why are you sitting in my chair? Dennis was the number one high school receiver in Florida coming out of high school. He could have gone anywhere. I know Hugh Green, a fabulous linebacker who won the Lombardi Award, was Dennis's chaperone when he visited Pitt. Dennis got one taste of the cold weather and decided to cross Pitt off his list."

The subject of Dennis's recruitment still obviously rankles the coach.

"I just wish Dennis had chosen a school that would have made better use out of him in the passing game. I'll also tell you this, Miami was stupid. Dennis was playing right next door to the 'Canes, right by the campus, and they didn't recruit him. He was the number one receiver in the state of Florida as a senior, the number two receiver in America overall, and Miami just looked the other way. It was out and out stupid."

Dennis returns to South Miami High.

"Did I mention that coach Marc used to get on my case about blocking? I'd tell him I catch the ball, I run the ball, I return punts and kickoffs, and I kick off and handle place kicks. When have I got time to block? I know Marc had a thought about make me a running back, but I didn't want my face to get busted up taking out a linebacker. Coach had told me that if I played running back, I'd have to block. If I had done that, I wouldn't have left South Miami High as the number one wide out in the state after my final season. I doubt my mom would have liked it either. Mom would yell like crazy, screaming "That's my baby" during my high school games. She's the only person I've ever seen who could yell like crazy with a mouth full of popcorn."

The subject of his mom brings another smile to Silky's face.

"You know my mom and Don Shula, then head coach of the Dolphins, knew each other. Mom used to drive the bus for the rich kids from Coral Gables High School, the team we loved to beat, to the Orange Bowl where their school band played at halftime. Coach Shula would always acknowledge Mom. Even if it was just a wave in passing, you knew they respected each other. You ask if it hurt me to see Mama driving the bus for the kids of wealth? Maybe a little, but my Southern Baptist upbringing helped me out. Plus, Mama had great pride in what she did. She knew she commanded respect, respect that was earned.

As for me, riding on that bus with the team I loved to beat up was a thrill. Here I am, a young kid in the historic Orange Bowl. Of course, I was in awe. I had a dream that someday I would be good enough to play for the Miami Dolphins. I settled for getting to know guys like Mercury Morris and Nat Moore and later, Dan Marino."

It's not like this area never received notoriety. After all, Baseball Hall of Famer Andre Dawson attended nearby Southwest High School. Andre is married to Vanessa, who was the Homecoming Queen the year South Miami Senior High School opened in 1972. But still, I asked if the guys on Dennis's high school team were jealous of Dennis's star power and notoriety.

"No, I never really felt a bit of it. Marc will tell you I was humble, a little bit shy, but I did pick up things rapidly. People might say I was the coach's pet, but again, I was doing so many things for our club, wearing so many hats, that comments like that would seem natural. There's another reason why there was no jealousy. I had grown up with so many of these kids. I knew so many of them since they were three years old. We all knew each other's moms. They trusted me and knew I was always willing to help. Respect was our code."

### 

There was another McKinnon that made an impact on the football fields of Florida. He was also a wrestler.

"I remember a match Donald (McKinnon) had with a kid from a rival high school," coach Marc recalls. "The kid was huge, a great wrestler, and he beat Donald. Now, the referee brings both boys to the center of the mat to raise the winner's hand. The ref raises this kid's hand and Donald was so upset that he slugged the guy right in the face. True story. Donald just said, 'I can't stand losing.'"

Coach Marc Paskow, Dennis and Donald's high school mentor and father figure, explained the connection between the two McKinnons.

"Donald was Dennis's cousin and really his role model. Donald was an interesting kid. When I began dealing with him, he was a sophomore, a chubby kid, who couldn't do a pushup. The first thing he told me was that he's going to set the school record in the bench press. I told him quit wasting time, go to work. Well, by the time he was senior, the chubby kid was benching 475 pounds."

Understand that Marc's a New Jersey guy through and through. He wouldn't tell a kid, well let's start slowly and work our way up. No chance. He would tell a youngster to quit messing around and hit the gym—hard.

"Donald had a presence," coach Marc recalls. "I remember one time during a study hall or a free period I was assigned to keep an eye on kids to make sure they were in class. I saw these two girls slugging it out. I mean they were really going at each other. I walked up to break the fight up when I got a tap on my shoulder. It was Donald. He told me, 'Coach, just step back, we'll handle this.' He settled the matter in just a few seconds."

Donald was a tremendous weight lifter and football player. He was an All-State football player who went to Eastern Kentucky on a full ride. Wally Chambers, a wicked ballplayer during the post Butkus-Sayers era with the Bears, also went to E.K.U. Wally was monster at defensive tackle. So good that he was chosen NFC defensive lineman of the year in 1976. However, he paid a heavy price for his energy on the grid. The past decade or so, Chambers has spent most of his time in a wheelchair or with a walker. The carpet at Soldier Field did him no favors.

"Sadly, we lost Donald when he was just 19," coach Marc says. "He passed away from spinal meningitis. He had been in the hospital, but the staff that treated him seemed to think he just had the flu or a cold. I remember I cried my eyes out at his funeral. It was the first time I had attended a funeral in an all-black neighborhood. Donald was one of a kind. It just crushed me when I saw Donald lying in his open coffin."

I asked the coach how Donald and Dennis compared as athletes.

"It's funny," Paskow says, "Dennis and I were lying on the beach few days ago. He looks tremendous. I told my wife he could still play. Dennis was the better athlete. He was so dedicated to blocking. He also loved to nail people on the blind side."

# Chapter Nine

Autumn has arrived. On a partly cloudy day with temps in the upper 50s and low 60s, Silky D and I settle in for lunch. There's no way we can avoid the biggest topic in Chicago football these days. As we take our usual corner table, I bring up the kid quarterback. His coach Nagy was saying that Trubisky played a good game versus New England. Remarkably ESPN's Mike Wilbon, a guy I love, said Mitch had played three straight great games. I was wondering if Silky agreed.

"I think mentally Trubisky played well, but that doesn't change the fact that while he was picked twice, New England also dropped two more picks in the end zone. People don't understand this and they should. The press and the Bears have put Mitch on a pedestal. Hear me out, it's hard to get better, it's hard to make anybody better, if they're not afraid of being benched. Think about the Trubisky Hail Mary at the gun which White caught at its highest point, then think about this. Why didn't Nagy have Mitch heave the ball to the end zone as time ran out before half time? It just made sense. Instead, Nagy had Trubisky throw under coverage to Tarik Cohen. All that play did was pad Cohen's stats and, of course, Trubisky's stats. You know, looking back on the game, if New England hadn't fumbled twice in the second quarter in its own territory, the Pats would have blown the Bears out."

I ask Silky what Trubisky should work on during the offseason and will he ever be an elite, or even very good, vertical passer?

"One, he needs to get rid of his beard! Seriously, Mitch has got to improve in 2019 because he will be called upon to shoulder more of the load. I would tell him this, get your hands on every tape you can of Tom Brady. Study Brady's ability to dictate to defenses. Watch Tom's pre-snaps read and how he moves various players to positions before the snap. Brady is great, tremendous, and he really doesn't have any gifted speed receivers. Basically, he's throwing to white guys. If Brady can work his magic with no real inside or outside speed, how good should Trubisky be with the receivers Bears fans rave about? Also, Matt Nagy has to recognize that teams will have the offseason to work on shutting down Trubisky when he runs on third down. There will be a linebacker spy on Mitch all next season. Teams will try to shut down his running ability and force him to be a pocket passer. Now, this is big, Trubisky will never be a great downfield passer. The deep ball is his Achilles heel. Then again, he isn't surrounded by great deep threats."

Silk and I started discussing some of the other players on the roster. First up, Allen Robinson, one of several new wide outs on the 2018 Bears.

"Last year at Jacksonville, this guy blew his knee out, tore his ACL, in the season opener against Houston. The Jags didn't tag him with the franchise or transition label. So the Bears sign him to a 42-million-dollar deal knowing full well it can take two years to fully recover from an ACL. Have you really felt his presence? Plus, he doesn't play on special teams. You have to ask—what is the return on the investment?"

What about Leonard Floyd and Roquan, I ask Silk.

"Floyd was a wasted draft pick. He's been given a free pass because he played on lousy teams and this year he hasn't been critiqued since all the attention has been thrust on Khalil Mack. Mack makes everybody on that defense look better. I'm not gonna get excited because Floyd had two fourth-quarter sacks against Rodgers. The sacks Floyd got on Aaron are what football players call garbage sacks.

As for Roquan, his speed against the run is tremendous, but he's still confused in coverage. He doesn't have bad footwork; he just doesn't understand the passing game. Let's just say that neither Floyd nor Roquan will ever compare to Wilber and to a lesser degree Otis Wilson.

Now, let's be hypothetical. Let's suppose that K. Mack was a middle linebacker, a 'Mike.' Would I take him over Mike Singletary? No, I wouldn't. Mike was Buddy Ryan on the field. Mack only has one motor. His job is to win at the line of scrimmage and rush the passer. While people rave about Khalil, if you watch closely, isolate 52, you will see he's human. He does make mistakes. Khalil is thought of as a one-trick pony. He's not. He's very solid against the run, but here again, his primary job is to rush the passer."

I mention to Silk that the buzz around Bears safety Eddie Jackson is overwhelming. For the record, and this goes back to the days of JFK, Eddie's strides remind me of former Bears defensive back Roosevelt Taylor. Rosey was a gazelle that seemed to take six feet between every stride. He was a hero and a half to me.

"Eddie Jackson is having a great year regardless of the weak competition the Bears have faced. His stats will earn him a spot in the Pro Bowl. But, hold on for a second, don't compare him to Dave Duerson or Mike Brown. Due and Mike played on a different level."

I bring up Prince Amukamara, the Bears defensive back. He has his priorities in some kind of order…just what that order is, I have no idea. Prince told the *Chicago Tribune*'s Brad Biggs that the defense loves to score touchdowns so it can show off its personality.

"Prince, the Bears were 5-11 last year, so just where was his 'personality' hiding?" Dennis asks. "Let me tell you what a guy like Walter Payton would say to this kid, there is nothing wrong with saying no comment. Pump your brakes, Prince. The Bears are in first place for the first time in, like, forever, so they're overjoyed to show their arrogance. There are too many football players today trying to bring back *Soul Train* or make themselves look like hip hop stars. A little celebrating is cool, but you've got clubs who are clearly on the practice field working on new routines. Most of the stuff looks stupid. Take a look at our '85 team. We won the division by seven games. That's when you can strut."

Meanwhile, Kyle Long, the former number one draft choice, now lists his home address as the whirlpool C.O. Halas Hall. I could list all of Kyle's injuries, but we're limited to 85,000 words. Listen, the guy is coming up on his 30th birthday. Is it time for the Bears to move on without Howie Long's 316-pound baby boy?

"The Bears can't trust their $10,000,000 guard," Silky says. "Look at the guards we had back in '85 when we won the Super Bowl. Tom Thayer and Mark Bortz were tremendous. They were also unsung heroes. Thayer was a member of a very exclusive club at Halas Hall, the "500 Club." What that means is he could bench press 500 pounds. Write this. Kyle Long simply isn't a player who matches up to Thayer or Mark. Not even close! I saw where the Bears restructured his contract. That's just not a good move. They should have cut his ass, he can't stay on the field. But Kyle is a company man, so the Bears took care of him. Check his numbers. The guy has only started 25 games the last three years."

Meanwhile, Charles Leno, is there any chance you can take that ring back to the jeweler? Shortly after the Bears disposed of the guys from the northland, Leno, on one knee, proposed to his long-time squeeze Jennifer Roth on the Soldier Field playing surface. Of course, the proposal created a terrestrial and social media frenzy. I immediately had visions of Charles and his fiancée working the couch with Kimmel, Fallon, and Ellen among others. But there is a twist to this yarn that isn't very pretty.

"Check out this girl's Twitter account," Dennis points out. "Her tweets are a disgrace. I'm sure she has appeased Charles by telling him that these Twitter rants took place long ago and that she has either found God or come to respect African Americans. I would tell her this: white girls sleeping with black guys doesn't give you the right to call them niggas."

Joe Fan has the misguided notion that this was a joyful, once-in-a-lifetime moment of giddiness and celebration. That doesn't play. You have to know that George McCaskey, Ted Phillips, Ryan Pace, Matt Nagy, and the entire Bears offensive line had to know what was going to go down. First off, fans aren't allowed on the field, so she had to be escorted down from the stands. That's just one phase of an occurrence that wasn't spontaneous—it was completely produced and orchestrated.

Now, we begin to examine the tweets of the so-called fiancée. You pick up on comments like "mixed babied niggas and niggas clowning" or, try this one, "Ghetto people are always naming their kids after stuff they can't afford 'Mercedes, Diamond, Bentley, Pearl.'"

So I know what the house wants to know. How are Leno's teammates going to react?

"The players are a fraternity. They will support Charles unless this issue becomes a distraction. If Leno gets torn up, he gives up a couple of sacks, he becomes a distraction. As a rule, distractions don't last long in this league. Plus, there is the female factor. Football teams have alpha males, and in turn there are alpha females. Females who love to talk. How will the ladies, wives and girlfriends of Bears players, react to Roth as more information is gathered?

I wish Wilber Marshall was here. I was the best man at Wilber's wedding. Things were a little uncomfortable. I knew the girl Wilber was marrying had her eyes on his paycheck. I flat out told my brother, don't marry this girl. Here's one thing that tipped me off that this woman was bad news. The girl had accrued about $36,000 in debt. Wilber covered all the bad tabs for her. Plus, he bought her almost $40,000 in jewelry around Christmas time. Was the woman grateful? Hardly, she said to Wilber—no kidding—'I really had my eyes set on a nice pair of earrings.' I knew then who she really was."

###

Some three hours into our lunch-bunch session, the NFL announced Pro Bowl selections. The Bears, who had been barren for far too long, had five players named to the squad led by K. Mack. Akiem Hicks, Kyle Fuller (my choice as NFL comeback player of the year), and Tarik Cohen will play in the ballgame nobody really wants to play in to begin with. Everyone wants to be voted in, but as for playing, well, the sandy beach of Maui or Cabo San Lucas are far more inviting. We aren't done yet. Somehow, Leonard Floyd, who spent most of the year in witness protection, was chosen as an alternate along with six other Bears: Trubisky, Trevathian, Burton, Whitehair, noted romantic Charles Leno, and, check the ballot box, Roquan Smith, who was a bust the first 11 weeks, maybe 12.

"Every defensive player selected should give Mack their Pro Bowl bonus," Dennis says. "His presence and disruption made this the best defensive in the league while playing a terribly weak schedule. Inspector Gadget (Tarik Cohen) doesn't have a lot of snaps, but he does make plays. If the Bears had not been winners, he's probably not selected. Winning always give you bonus votes. As for Leonard Floyd, don't make me throw up. His garbage sacks make it appear that he had a decent year. D-coordinators aren't scheming to stop Leonard Floyd. The NFC is terrible, it hasn't been this bad in years, and if Mack hadn't joined the Bears, Floyd would still be a ghost. The bar for the Pro Bowl is one heck of a lot lower than it used to be.

I will never watch the Pro Bowl again. I'd rather play marbles. The game is hapless, pathetic, about as engaging as watching a chess tournament. Sadly, I can recall a time when guys worked out hard to prepare for the so-called all-star game. They played all out as if the game was on the schedule in mid-October. Those days are so far in the rearview mirror they may as well be locked in a vault in Schenectady. Genuine, balls-out tackling or blocking is strictly forbidden."

"Here's the first major problem," Dennis points out. "The Pro Bowl used to be played after the Super Bowl so the league had a fighting chance at getting most of its top players to compete. Now, as a fill-in game between Conference Championship Sunday and the Super Bowl, the league is just trying to fill out rosters. The game is about social media and hashtags."

What does Silky think about Coach Nagy?

"Keep this in mind," Dennis opines. "The league will catch up with Matt Nagy's offense. Here's what I can tell you about Matt Nagy. He hasn't shown me yet that he's a big game coach. So far, I'd give him a 'B.' Nagy is great with the press, he fills up the notepads. Of course, after Lovie Smith, Marc Trestman, and John Fox, he had no act to follow. Fox was a mute. Right now, Nagy is under no threat. He's stolen a page from the Joe Maddon playbook and has his guys dancing in the locker room after home wins. Wait, you're dancing when you're 4 and 3 and you haven't beaten a quality team? I can tell you this about Nagy. He's a better friend to his players than he is a coach. That's okay as long as you get your players to buy into your system. I'm not being negative. That's not me. I state facts."

### 

I wondered how Silk felt about the painful playoff loss. First of all, what was his take on the Bears sending out Dick Butkus and Brian Urlacher to rev up the crowd before the Bears and Eagles kicked off?

"Typical," Silk responds. "Where are all the gold jackets? You know what I saw? Howie Long sitting in the press box waiting for his kid Kyle to come up with his next ankle injury. Meanwhile our '85 champs can't buy their way into the ballpark."

Let's talk about that ending and its aftermath. Parkey clanks the boot while the press clobbers the woebegone kicker.

"Kickers are enigmatic with personality disorders," Dennis says. "When they're on the field you're always rolling the dice."

A little history. As a reporter I covered my first Bears game in 1969, 50 years ago. I have seen the Bears lose games that were so brutal, so mind-altering, that people who should know better were dying to autograph their throats with switchblades or at least double up on Xanax.

However, in a half century of pontificating about the NFL's most unique and enigmatic franchise, I have never witnessed a defeat as crushing as the Bears 16-15 playoff loss to the Eagles. So sudden, so draining. Imagine walking into a wake with 60,000 people.

In case you've been in New Zealand or a federal pen, let me give you a primer. With time running out on the lakefront, Parkey lined up for a very makeable field goal of 43 yards. He nailed the kick, slammed it right down the main drag, but it meant nothing. Philly coach Doug Pederson had called for time with one second left on the play clock to "ice" Parkey.

Actually, icing kickers began around the 1915, so Parkey had time to think as he approached his second try. Did he talk himself into a miss? Did an Eagle defender get just enough of the ball to veer it off course? If you don't feel Parkey's pain, you're heartless. Then again, there are other opinions.

"I don't feel sorry for Parkey at all," former Bears kicker Kevin Butler told me. "These days if you aren't kicking at about an 85 percent rate, your ass is on the street. Parkey really had a bad year."

Parkey missed. The kid missed. Sadly, it will certainly be Cody's NFL legacy. Thirty years from now people will still be pounding him about the loss to Philly. Cody, a stand-up guy, is now cursed just as Bill Buckner was given a lifetime scarlet letter back in '86 when he fumbled a ninth inning ground ball off the bat of Mookie Wilson that allowed the Mets to beat the Red Sox in game six of the World Series.

"The well ran dry," Dennis says. "The finality shouldn't have surprised anybody who looked at just how the Bears fattened up on the weakest schedule in the NFL."

Kickers are Bipolar...they're special needs kids. I was disgusted by the fan response on Twitter, death threats by drunken Monday morning quarterbacks who will tell you after they sober up, "Oh, I was drinking." In case you missed it, football players have wives and families.

It takes guts to be a kicker. Unless you played the game, you have no idea, you can't conceive the pressure these guys are under or for that reason all NFL players are under. It's easier now with so much guaranteed money, but it still requires a special kind of person to reach the NFL, let alone last in the NFL.

I asked Silk if he was disgusted—especially as a guy who played the game—when the local media, most notably the Trib and Sun Times, all but ignored the NFL's statement that the Parkey kick was "officially" blocked. A couple of fingers, even a single digit grazing the ball, can move the rock five degrees off course and create a miss.

"The press overlooked the fact that Parkey was also an All Pro at Philadelphia. They overlooked that he joined his teammates and members of the Eagles in a postgame prayer before leaving the field to a chorus of four-letter words. The media had formed its narrative. Here was this 5 and 11 club in '17 that became new age darling this season. In their minds, Parkey spoiled their story line. The media will never forgive him for spoiling their joy ride. Let me send this message to fans:

If you never wore pads, if you never got a game check from the NFL, keep quiet and sit in the cheap seats."

Cody Parkey has been hit more times than Joe Frazier was smacked the first time he fought George Foreman.

"Shit happens," Dennis says. "Receivers drop passes, quarterbacks fumble snaps, and left tackles miss blocks. I would tell Parkey's teammates this: Cody was one of your brothers. The Bears didn't really protect him as a teammate, as a brother."

For the most part, the local media in Chicago remains hysterical because a professional athlete accepted an invitation to appear on a national TV show that debuted, good morning, 67 years ago, when America was watching 8- and 12-inch black and white TVs with rabbit ears as big as 3-irons. The Bears' brass was something less than thrilled, make that disgusted, about Parkey doing his TV shot.

"Why shouldn't Cody do *The Today Show*?" Dennis asks. "And ask yourself another question. What's the big deal? Now, how would a local media that blatantly plays favorites have treated Mitch Trubisky if he'd thrown a pick in the final minute of play against the Eagles that cost the Bears the ballgame? They would have cut him all the slack in the world.

I never heard about guys needing permission to go on national television, when did that rule get put in place? After we beat the Giants in the 1985 playoffs, I did *Good Morning America* with a patch over my eye. Two weeks later I did the Ted Koppel show before Super Bowl XX. The Koppel show wanted 'Fridge' but he was off on a Bourbon Street prowl, so I got his chair. In both cases, I didn't ask or need for any form of permission."

If you're Parkey, why wouldn't you take the chance to tell you story on *Today*? Is he supposed to grieve, go into mourning for six months, before he talks about the clank? Leave the guy alone."

(Note: The Bears, as expected, eventually unloaded Parkey on March 13, the first day of the NFL's new calendar year.)

# Chapter Ten

The weather seemed to have a way of taking care of Dennis and me. Whenever we gathered at our favorite Northfield hangout for one of our bull sessions, the sun invariably was shining. However, when Dennis walked in I could tell by looking at his forehead if he was in an upbeat mood or ready to tear into something that had left him disgusted. Today he flashed me his dazzling smile. I thought it would be a good day to walk down memory lane.

Dennis, you had to be a big man in the high school hallways, right?

"Early on I was a little bit shy," Dennis says, "but people did find me likeable. I was never a troublemaker or a guy who tried to be a hot shot. But as I advanced through school and became a so-called football hero, people really did begin to gravitate to me, and I began to eliminate my shyness factor. I still smile when I think about my girlfriend Kathy Ervin, the captain of the cheerleading squad, wearing my letter sweater. Think about it, you're a high school kid, life is going so fast, it's still a series of confusing questions, but my girl wearing my sweater made me a big man on campus."

This young damsel sounds intriguing. Play on, Silk.

"Kathy was the daughter of a pastor, so that meant I had to be a gentleman. She was just a gorgeous chocolate caramel girl. Her walk could stop traffic. She made me respect the guy who invented blue jeans. We were really hooked on each other, and eventually, in between listening to The Temptations, Marvin Gaye, The O'Jays, Aretha (Franklin), and Teddy Pendergrass, we both lost our virginity when we were around 17 years old."

Did the experience live up to the buildup?

"Absolutely, but when it was over we were like, 'Finally, It's about time.' Kathy followed me to Florida State. I guess we thought we might get married, but our love affair fizzled over time when we both discovered there were a lot more men and women in the world. Temptation got the best of us, as it does with so many young kids."

### 

The subject turns to basketball. Hoops time, lay the wood on LeBron! As we spoke, LeBron was just weeks away from passing Michael Jordan on the all-time scoring list.

"LeBron didn't go to college," Dennis points out. "He jumped right to the NBA. Where would Michael be if he had gone from high school to the NBA and he hadn't walked away from the NBA for a year and half to play baseball? To me, James is self-absorbed. He was good, but not great, before he went to Miami and hooked up with Dwayne Wade. On his own James couldn't really flourish, but in Miami he found a willing wingman. D. Wade had enough class and personal resolve to take a back seat to James, so the so-called king was the Heat's primary scoring option. Dwayne knew that James would pout if he didn't get the touches, the points he wanted."

And how many pout more about fouls?

"Tell me how many guys in the NBA who are 6'8" and weigh 270 pounds flop like LeBron does? Here is my Mount Rushmore. I can't talk about Wilt (Chamberlain), Oscar Robertson, or Bill Russell because I just never saw them play. So I'll got one through five with M.J., Magic Johnson, Shaq (O'Neal), Larry Bird, Hakeem Olajuwon, and Tim Duncan, the most underrated and underappreciated player of my era, and finally LeBron James."

With that Dennis and I begin to talk about our mutual dislike for the style of ball the NBA plays these days and the untimely deaths of so many youthful R&B and rock singers. Silky and I are more or less in accord that the Motown Hall of Fame begins with Marvin Gaye, former Temptations lead singer David Ruffin and his running mate Eddie Kendricks, who provided so many Temps' songs with their unique falsetto sound, and no doubt, Michael Jackson. As an added attraction we also throw in Rick James, the "Super Freak," who primarily recorded off Motown subsidiary (Barry) Gordy records.

"You can't help but wonder why so many artists die so young," Dennis says. "Jimi Hendrix, Janis Joplin, Jim Morrison, Eddie and David, Amy Winehouse, Rick James. No doubt some were scooped up by the drug life, but what about the pressure to record, to sell, and to perform? Look at Michael Jackson, he wasn't raised a slave, but his father Joe made him a slave, treated him like a slave. Joe Jackson wanted his kid to turn out bubblegum crap like "Ben" and "Mama's Pearl" while Michael had the urge to grow.

Michael must have had 100 people on his payroll. If he didn't work, his entourage didn't get paid. It's no wonder he never slept. That creates enormous pressure and tension."

I told Dennis that I miss the NBA game when it was played inside out. I feel blessed that I saw Wilt Chamberlain, Bill Russell, Wes Unseld, Walt Bellamy, Patrick Ewing, Brad Daugherty, and Bill Laimbeer, the slime bucket head hunter, from the Detroit Pistons "Bad Boys" era. The Bulls' rivalries with the Pistons and Knicks were fierce. Guys could check with two hands. If you drove the lane you were going to pay a price. Even the officials, Eddie Rush, Earl "Yogi" Strom, and Dick Bavetta were far more colorful than today's zebras, and they maintained far better dialogue with the players and coaches. I still watch the NBA, but I am too often lulled to sleep by watching four guys stand outside the arc while one guy waits to set a screen.

Dennis has another issue with the game.

"I can't stand all the NBA players who flop. It's a way of life. Players rarely get teed up. I agree with you, there is just no interior play. I've also had my fill of players bitching about 'only' making 25 million a year."

###

I see the tab approaching. You'd think after a while they'd start comping us Dennis's Cokes and my Diet Cokes. I sense that Dennis has something he wants to say.

"Let me throw in a few things. Fans don't know this, but a lot of players with CTE are using marijuana. Why not? They're begging for some kind of emotional escape."

The subject of drugs is now on the table, so I ask him where he stands.

"People ask me all the time about cocaine use," he responds, "which is an insult. I've got better things to spend my money on. Two, a message I was taught at a very young age by my mama. No one, through disgust or temptation or slurs, should have the power to put you in a position to fail. Mama raised me to know better."

I've never seen Dennis with a drink in his hands. Has he ever been loaded?

There's a long pause before he answers.

"Just once," he finally says. "Years ago, I was at a party at one of Walter's places, the Pacific Club in Lombard. I must have had 12 Amaretto Stone Sours. It was my birthday and people were buying me drinks, shots, left and right. A cop pulled me over on my way home to Gurnee. After he took my license and registration—and I'm thinking the worst—he saw my name, and with the date, knew it was my birthday. He told me two things: Dennis, I'm surprised your friends would let you

81

drive home in the shape you're in. And secondly, I'm going to follow you home to make sure you get to your place safely. I learned a lesson that day. Lay off Goldschlager shots."

As long as we're tackling controversial subjects, I threw out another one. Where did Dennis stand on guns?

"I am vehemently opposed to the NRA," he says. "I have never owned a gun or shot a gun in my life. I have never wanted to be tempted by the devil. Why would you own a gun unless you're a hunter? Why the hell would I want an assault rifle? Young kids get lured by guns. They think it builds them up as a man, it builds up their street credit. It doesn't."

# Chapter Eleven

Between our conversations, I thought I would check in with a few of Dennis's former teammates and coaches. I thought it would be a great way to get a measure of the man, and it turns out I was right.

First call—current Bears radio analyst, and good ol' #57, Tom Thayer.

I love big old Tom Thayer, the pride and joy of Joliet Catholic High School and the University of Notre Dame. Tom anchored the left guard spot for the Bears during the gravy train years in the mid-1980s. He was big, tough, and brawny, a 271-pound hunk of muscle and determination with an upper I.Q. football intelligence. Though he never aggressively sought the spotlight, Tom was and is an enormously popular figure with Bears fans all over the country due to his take-no-prisoners style of play and, over the past two decades, his work as a Grade A color announcer on the Bears Radio Network with play by play man Jeff Joniak.

Think about this. You wonder how Thayer's body held up. Tom was drafted by Jim Finks and the Bears in 1983 but chose to sign with George Allen and the long-gone USFL Chicago Blitz for a very simple reason. The Blitz, who eventually became the Arizona Wranglers, gave Thayer guaranteed first round money while the Bears had projected Tom as a third or fourth round pick. Here's where it gets interesting. Double T played a full schedule, 20 games, with Arizona in '85 before joining the Bears, where he played all 16 regular season games and three playoff games. Perfunctory math. Thayer played 39 pro football games in one year, which if it isn't a record, sure as hell should be.

If you're curious, Tom is listed as a first teamer on the all-time all USFL team. Honestly, did you know there was an all-time USFL team?

Tom has nothing but praise for #85.

"Dennis wasn't just tough," Tom tells me, "he was a devastating downfield blocker. Silk would take on guys who outweighed HIM by 80 pounds and make THEM feel like HE outweighed them by 80 pounds. I respect Dennis the same way I respected Mike Tyson when Tyson was in his prime."

Dennis returned the praise when I relayed it to him.

"Tom was beyond durable," Silk points out. "Think about how many games he played that one year. It's just a feat that goes beyond incredible. He was the last piece of our puzzle that created an offensive line that was so mobile, with such quick feet and, of course, overwhelming power. Dick Stanfel, our offensive line coach, knew what he had and how to mold that offensive line into the machine, ball control unit, it became."

### 

It doesn't take long to recognize that Silky's former teammates recall a hard-nosed tough jock whose respect level has only grown with the passage of time. Take for example, Emery Moorehead, the cerebral tight end out of Evanston Township High School, who will tell you that in today's NFL Dennis might catch 100 balls a year. I caught up with E at his winter home in Colorado where he's comfortably in retirement.

"You have to remember, back in the 80s we were a strict, run-oriented football team," Emery points out. "We were built around Walter. We weren't running five wide. Our job was to keep the defense off the field, and we did that to perfection. We've never been given the credit we really deserve. I remember mini-camp in '83, the year Dennis arrived with that great class of rookies. A reporter pulled me aside and asked me which guy impressed me the most, I told him keep an eye on

85 (Dennis's number). He really wants to play football. Here we had all this talent, just a great rookie class of talent, and I'm raving about a free agent. Ditka loved Dennis for at least one reason. He'd stick his nose in a guy's gut. He didn't hesitate to use his body. There just wasn't another receiver in the NFL who blocked with the effectiveness that Dennis did. He was the physically toughest wide out in the game."

"When I joined the Bears," Dennis says, in response to Emery's comments, "Ted Plumb, our receivers coach, knew we had to change the way we ran the ball. We just weren't getting to the second level. Ted sold us, got us to commit to blocking downfield. That's what earned me my job with the Bears."

###

I asked Dennis about the kicker on his championship Bears team. It's not often you get a non-kicker to say such nice things about a kicker.

"That's because our kicker Kevin Butler was a different breed," Silk tells me. "He had the mentality of a linebacker. I can still see him selling out, putting his body on the line to make tackles on kickoffs. Kevin had no fear, absolutely none. You know kickers have to fight for respect. Butt-head wasn't accepted in our locker room the day he showed up. He had to prove he had balls. Our teams knew how to circle the wagons, we did circle the wagons and Butt-head was very much a part of that circle. There is no kicker today who plays the game the way Kevin did. You just don't see kickers today play with Butler's kind of attitude."

Butler used to call the Kevin Matthews show on the legendary LOOP AM-1000 and spend maybe a half hour talking back and forth with Kev—while the rest of the team was practicing! Butler was at once a hell raiser with veins that were ice blue. His timing was perfect. After a brilliant career kicking for Vince Dooley at Georgia, Butler joined the

Bears just in time to win a ring in Super Bowl XX. He famously called his fiancé Cathy during training camp in the summer of '85 to tell her that they had to postpone their wedding set for late January because the Bears were going to win a Super Bowl. I'd love to know what Cathy's reaction was when Kevin said put a hold on the caterer and the flowers, because this team is gonna win the bundle.

This is remarkable, think about this. Over 11 years with the Bears, he never had a kickoff returned for a touchdown. I saw him take down Deion Sanders, Barry Sanders, and Mel Gray more than once when Kev was the last body left in front of the end zone.

When I called Butt-Head, we began reflecting about the Bears 21-0 playoff win over the Giants during the '85 year of glamour.

"Thank God Dennis had two touchdown catches," he said with a laugh, "because with the wind I missed three field goals."

### 

Don't ask me why, but I had suddenly felt the urge to call Johnny Roland, a truly versatile football player, who coached Bears' running backs under Mike Ditka from 1983 to 1992. J.R. was a running back in the early 60s at Missouri when single platoon football (no free substitution) was still in vogue. In other words, a whole heck of a lot of guys were 60-minute players. Roland was terrific for Mizzou during his first year with the Tigers, but ironically, he became a College All-American in '66 as a defensive back!

He was also the first black athlete to be chosen captain of any team sport at Missouri.

He later played seven years with the old St. Louis Cardinals and a windup season with the New York Giants. I loved it when Johnny was with the Bears. Much like Ted Plumb and later Dave McGinnis, he was a fountain of information, info I never really used, because John and I shared a bond that what we discussed was off the record.

"Dennis was uncanny," Johnny told me. "He wasn't afraid to take a guy head on or go over the middle. Dennis didn't have any fear, and the Bears got him for next to nothing. You know Walter Payton just loved Silky. Sweetness knew that Dennis churned and burned for him downfield. Walter had such admiration for Dennis's absolute commitment. Of course, Silky could have caught significantly more balls if he had played with another team. That has to hurt him. Dennis McKinnon was grossly underrated. He was the fly-under-the-radar guy who drove other teams nuts. I saw him leave Lawrence Taylor bewildered in our '85 playoff game with the Giants."

As the running backs coach, Johnny knew how important Dennis was to the team's running game.

"Dennis was a major cog on a team that basically earned its living running the football. Our defense was fabulous, but our offense kept them off the field by moving the chains. Mike (Ditka) instilled a beat-the-hell-out-of-them mentality with our offense. I firmly believe that our '85 club was, for one year, the greatest team in NFL history."

Johnny agrees with me that coaches staying until midnight in darkened rooms looking at the same play 200 times is nuts. If you don't see where your plays will work after a dozen reads, you become a one-man poker game. Remember the old adage that defines great poker players from chip losers, if you can't spot the sucker in your first 30 minutes at the table you are the sucker.

"I'm one of the people who believe Dennis could have been a very good NFL coach," Roland says. "Sure, he had a wild child spirit about him, but I don't doubt that he could have channeled himself to the commitment necessary to coach. I do know this, Dennis would not have been another Dick Vermeil, a guy I coached under at Philadelphia. Dick would keep the staff up until 2 o'clock in the morning to talk about one play—off tackle."

I mentioned Johnny's opinion to Dennis.

"Coaching takes a lot of patience. Today's players don't want practice or coaching. They want highlights on YouTube. It's a different era. Film has given way to iPads. Perfection is no longer demanded."

Dennis has fond memories of his days with Johnny Roland.

"I can still see Johnny in his sweat suit, perspiring like crazy coaching up Walter, Matt Suhey, and the other guys who were cogs in our running game. He was so dedicated."

Just as Johnny reveres McKinnon, I will always have a very soft spot for Johnny Roland.

###

Ted Plumb was born with heart of gold. If you don't like this gentle and kind-hearted man who was born in Reno, Nevada, you just don't like people.

Ted's coaching career stretches back to 1962 when he was surely earning nickels and dimes coaching on the high school and junior college level. Plumb got his "door opener" break when he joined the New York Giants in 1974. Along the way, Ted would become what so many coaches become: a travelin' man with stops in Atlanta, Philadelphia, Arizona, and two tours with the Bears, 1980 thru '85 and later in 1996-'97.

After a brief stint in 1999-2000 as Director of Pro Personnel for the old St. Louis Cardinals with Marshall Faulk, Isaac Bruce, and Kurt Warner during an era when the club picked up billing as "The Greatest Show on Turf," Ted retired to his home in Alba, Texas. Alba is something less than a metropolis. A 2010 census listed the population at 504 residents. However, the little berg is just 86 miles from Kilgore,

Texas, where a spectacular park now stands on what used to be the richest oil developing property in the world. No, I don't know how many stoplights Alba has. Maybe two or three?

Simply put, I love Ted Plumb, while Ted, in turn, may well be the unofficial president of the Dennis McKinnon fan club.

"Dennis was one of the most effective players I ever coached," he tells me. "The first time I saw him in camp in 1983 I knew he was a winner. He was such an excellent blocker because he took so much pride in what he did. Perhaps, more than anyone else on our team, he appreciated the fact that he was leading a path for Walter Payton. Dennis's football intelligence was just tremendous. He also might be as tough as any guy I've ever been around."

Dennis returns the love.

"Ted taught me a great deal about football, especially about reading defenses since I was in motion so often, which allowed me to scan the field. Ted also knew what he had in me if the Bears were going to win. Willie (Gault) was limited in what he could bring to the club. I really believe Ted went a long way in terms of making me a special player. I had to get used to blocking defensive ends (at 182 pounds soaking wet), linebackers, safeties, and from time to time nose guards if I had to motion inside for a wham block.

Here's a prime example. We were lined up in a flop formation and I was splitting the difference between Willie and Jimbo Covert. I noticed a defensive guy rolling up to the line of scrimmage. I knew we were outnumbered on protection, so I shifted down to Jimbo so I could get a chip on the guy on my way out of the play."

Just like Ted Plumb taught him.

# Chapter Twelve

Pro football 1985 marked the Bears' 66th year in the football business. Few remembered or cared to note that the beloved Papa Bear, George Halas, the club's longtime owner and, for 40 years split over four tenures of 10 years each, the team's head coach, had kept the league alive during the great depression and World War II through sheer will.

As the calendar moved from spring to summer, the buildup surrounding the '85 Bears became almost suffocating. Auto dealers, shopping centers, and taverns all wanted a piece of the Bears. By mid-season, the Bears were no longer a football team, they were rock stars, the Beatles arriving in America. I recall Silky, Dan Hampton and me doing an appearance at the long-gone Ultimate Sports Bar and Grill in Lincoln Park. The joint was mobbed. The place was a living, breathing violation of the city's fire code. As the three of us talked to the audience, there had to be about 200 people outside in near-zero weather just staring through the windows to get a glimpse of da two Bears.

The '85 club dripped with charisma, funk, and a big slice of country style livin'. I have always maintained that guys like me who actively covered the Bears should have paid for the privilege of reporting on this gridiron version of the Ringling Bros. and Barnum & Bailey Circus. Today, the 1985 season would be our main topic of discussion.

Dennis starts off with an important point.

"Here is something football fans don't know because they've never been educated about it. If an offense goes on an extended, 15-play, 82-yard drive to score, it's exhausting. Your concentration and physical exertion are going nonstop for seven, eight, maybe nine minutes. I know I've been there. Plus, in my case there was another element in the mix. I returned punts. So after a drive I'd get to the bench, sip some Gatorade, and then really I had to stay ready. I couldn't take the proverbial deep breath. If our opponent was looking at second and long, I had to have my helmet on and be ready to go. Because in about 45 seconds I could be back on the field to return a punt.

You'll never get our defense to talk about this point. There were plenty of times when we'd start with the ball around the 18-yard line and our defense just knew we'd string together a long seven-minute drive, an extended drive. They could take their helmets off and chill. That's never talked about when people reflect on our '85 club. Sometimes the best defense is a good offense, in our case an offense that leads the NFL in rushing and time of possession."

McKinnon played on guts in '85. His left knee was getting drained and shot every two weeks. The Bears employed common sense in December and shut Silk down for two games to get him ready for the playoffs. What about the division? Forget about it! For all practical purposes the Bears had clinched the division a week before Columbus Day. There's a reason why they felt confident enough to do "The Super Bowl Shuffle" so early in the season. Of course, that song is a touchy subject with Dennis.

"I still wonder why Willie Gault left me out of 'The Super Bowl Shuffle.' We used to be brothers. Perhaps it reflects on Cain and Abel. Cain killed his brother; Willie knows he cut me deeply by shutting me out of the shuffle. That being said, I have heard so much about 'The Super Bowl Shuffle' over the years that it makes my skin crawl. But I don't hold a grudge. I still respect Willie. Grudges will only make you grow old, withdrawn, and bitter. You have to move on with life."

Super Bowl XX will always be special, but it will also always be a bit raw for Dennis. I want to stand back, keep quiet, and let Dennis play this round solo.

"Being shutout and not targeted in that Super Bowl still hurts me. I think about all the work I put in, the cortisone shots I absorbed without complaint, just to get to the big dance on national and international TV, and then not having the ball thrown my way...yes, it hurts.

I was perpetually injured, but I played. I had a great season. I led the Bears in scoring with nine touchdowns, and I led the club in postseason scoring. What was my reward? Willie Gault was showcased, the Willie Gault who lived in fear of going over the middle or sticking his head in a guy's gut. There were no endorsements for me. Let's face it, I was, and am, charismatic. I could have danced on Soul Train. I was asked to guest on Miami Vice but had to turn down the request because I had knee surgery and I was on crutches.

It seems like politics hit me straight in the face and I found out just how much the Bears, the NFL, and the game itself could control how much money I was going to earn. The politics cost me a great deal of money I could have made without the luxury of free agency. One knows getting to the Super Bowl is a privilege and you have to make the most of the opportunity. After 1985 we just never got back.

The hurt will always be there.

After we won the Super Bowl, I asked the Bears if my mom could fly with us on the charter back to Chicago. They said no. I was livid. My mom and her girls had been bringing us post-game meals to the Big Sombrero in Tampa after every game we'd played there. I mean, she really worked hard.

My teammates loved her.

Mom would cook soul food, ribs, collard greens, macaroni and cheese, the whole nine yards. So get this. After we won the Super Bowl and you know, doubled the value of the franchise, and established a whole new form of marketing in the NFL, the Bears told my mom she wasn't good enough to fly on our charter.

Believe me, there were open seats. There always are.

All I could think of were the times my mom and her friends would show up at the ballpark in Tampa and park right next to our team bus and they would load the food on the bus for us to take back and eat on the plane. She did it from the heart."

# Chapter Thirteen

There were lots of highs and a few lows in Dennis's post-Super Bowl Bears career, and today we were determined to talk about them. For instance, you may or may not remember Dennis's 1986 season.

"So, shortly after we clobbered the Pats in the Super Bowl," Dennis says, "I went up to East Lansing, Michigan, to see noted surgeon Lanny Johnson. Lanny had done work on a number of players, most notably Walter. The first thing Lanny said to me was, 'I don't know how you played. Your knee is shot.' He told me I had two options. Play another year on my bad knee and my career is likely over, or have surgery, sit out a year, and come back fresh in 1987.

My thought process was simple. Why should I bust my ass for a club that wasn't paying me what I was worth and also dissed my mother? I knew the Bears had to pay me, so my decision was easy. Lanny performed surgery and I sat out all of '86."

That must have been hard to watch, I pointed out.

"No, I didn't get depressed during my year off," Dennis says with a grin. "I had, shall we say, great nurses and got to see life from a different perspective. I realized that I was done playing in pain. There was no reciprocity. I also spent time in '86 mentoring our receivers, guys like Ron Morris and even Willie (Gault). I had to protect my body."

Dennis wasn't the only one who sat out the 1986 season. So did Leslie Frazier. And so did the Honey Bears. They were sidelined forever after the Super Bowl.

"You know the Honey Bears were an extension of the Bears but not really part of the Bears," Dennis says. "I never talked about it with anybody. A lot of the cheerleaders thought they had marquee value because they were in their cute little outfits on the sidelines, but ask yourself, were the fans really paying any attention to them? I give them credit for this. When we played the Giants in January of '86, it was freezing outside. But they were still out there squealing, 'Let's get fired up—ooo-ahh.'

The girls made next to nothing to cheer on Sunday, but most of them did quite well with appearances. As our celebrity as a team grew in '84 and '85, the cheerleaders also grew in stature. Honey Bears were everybody's guests. When you'd see them in clubs, they never had to go near a check. They were, in their own way, stars. I was amazed when they got fired after we won the Super Bowl. Who were they bothering? You know when the Honey Bears were around the team, we had their backs. If a girl was getting hassled by some guy in a bar, we wouldn't hesitate to step in to tell the guy to get lost.

From that standpoint we genuinely respected them."

### 

I've often referred to the following quote from Lombardi when referencing a play we're about to chat about: "I firmly believe that any man's finest hour, the greatest fulfillment of all that he holds dear, is that moment when he has worked his heart out in a good cause and lies exhausted on the field of battle – victorious."

Opening night, 1987, McKinnon fields a punt from the Giants' Sean Landeta (the same guy who whiffed on a punt in a playoff game between the Bears and New York in '85). Silk is about to put on a display of acrobatics and athletics that leaves a full house at Soldier Field roaring so loudly you could hear them in Merrillville. Many fans were gasping.

It remains the greatest play I've ever seen by a Bear since the team made Soldier Field its permanent home in 1971. Students, be patient, we're leading up to Silky D's dramatics. Armchair quarterbacks, take note: Dennis had done this after three knee surgeries.

There was no love lost between the Giants and the Bears and in particular a string bean receiver from Halas Hall. In that '85 playoff game (actually January 1986), Silk got into it with Lawrence Taylor. You can build a strong case that by the mid-80s, L.T. had replaced Walter Payton as the face of the NFL.

So we arrive at September 14, 1987. Monday Night Football on the lakefront as the Bears open their 68th season. The tension was palpable. It was beyond a marquee matchup. The game had been built up for months as a showdown between the two previous Super Bowl champs, Ditka and the Bears and Bill Parcells and the Giants. The anticipation took on a vibe that seemed a great deal like Ali-Frazier 1 in Madison Square Garden back on March 8, 1971.

All the game was missing was the larger-than-life presence of Howard Cosell. Howard, who redefined the sports broadcasting landscape with his laconic "Tell it like it is" approach, had dropped off MNF several years earlier.

Dennis remembers that night well.

"All players will tell you they hate night games," he says. "You watch football Sunday, drive to the team hotel. You have a meeting on Monday morning and then the clock becomes your worst enemy. You have to shut down. You don't take phone calls. You just want to be left alone. Plus, in my case I wasn't the happiest camper in the world. (Mike) Ditka always preached that you couldn't lose your job due to injury. So why was Ron Morris on the field in my spot and I'm on the bench? I asked the week of the game if I could return punts.

So, the game moves to the third quarter and Sean Landeta reappears. Sean lifted a high, towering punt in my direction. It seemed like a 747. I could see that the point of the ball was facing downward, so I knew he had out-kicked the coverage. The first move I made was to my left to get the Giants' gunner on that side to commit. There were three Giants who had shot at me around the 30-yard line but never got ahold of me. You probably recall that I slipped up just a bit and almost hit the turf, but I was able to keep my balance and won the track meet to the end zone, 94 yards to the house. It was even a greater thrill than blowing up L.T."

The play remains etched in stone in my memory bank. If there was one word I would use to describe the effort, my choice would be 'bedazzling.'

"Understand part of my motivation," Dennis explains. "I figured I was running for my job. My first reaction when I got to the end zone was, ' I told you I could play, ya fuckers.' Did I mention the play covered 94 yards? Think about that—94 yards. You know Ditka always called me kid. I don't recall what he said to me—or if he said anything after my return—but I do recall later in the year that Mike said to me, 'Whatever the hell we owe you, we gotta pay you.'"

### 

Let's dig in with the historic "Fog Bowl," New Year's Eve 1988 at Soldier Field. I asked Dennis if he remembered Buddy (Ryan) having the Eagles team buses circle Soldier Field twice to let the Bears know they were in town.

"Yes, very much so," Dennis replies. "One guy on our club said he hoped Buddy choked on a Ditka pork chop. I did something before that game I can never recall having done before. I made a point to hug Ted Plumb, our former receivers coach, who was, of course, part of Buddy's staff. I loved Ted, and Ted wasn't the enemy. At the end of the day the game may be a business, but it's also about mutual respect and families.

By the way, I had signed a new three-year deal in '88 worth just under one million dollars. I really deserved about 1.4 mill. Willie Gault was gone and McMahon was a shadow of his former self. My value to the Bears had grown dramatically.

The fog was really uncharted waters for us as a ball club. We had never played in conditions like that before. As the waves of fog rolled in, we knew one thing for certain, we had to be a running team. I also want to mention that the Bears were playing their first regular season on natural grass after nearly two decades on Astroturf. Ironically, the previous season, 1987, was Walter's final year with the Bears."

Nevertheless, before Soldier Field looked like it had been covered with banana cream pie, you racked up the game's first score. Give the class the rundown. I will tell the house that the play covered 64 yards.

"I was lined up in the slot with Andre Waters, another player we lost to head trauma. Poor Andre took his own life in his Tampa home in 2006. T-Zak (Mike Tomczak) was our quarterback. I'm looking at Andre. If he blitzes, I become the hot read. If he stays back, I know he's in coverage. In an instant I knew he was going to drop back. Andre guessed wrong while he defended me and, in doing so, slipped. I actually had to wait for T-Zak to throw me the ball. It had to be the easiest TD catch of my NFL career.

By the way, after the game Mike Ditka did give me one of our game balls. I really believe that in 1988, I became the spiritual leader on our football team. Walter had walked away from the game, and Jim McMahon in his final year in Chicago only played nine games."

Mac had also written a fiery book about George Halas and the McCaskeys. Inside the book authored by *Tribune* columnist Bob Verdi, Jim also took his own parents to task for not showing his wife proper love. Kevin Butler told me a day or two after the book hit the street that he had knew Mac was gone.

"Ours is a funny world," Dennis says. "How many DUIs does Dan Hampton have? I'm not sure he even has a driver's license, but he endorses Chevrolets. Think about that. It's just too weird. No license, sell cars, WTF?"

I went down to the Soldier Field sidelines late in the second quarter as the fog engulfed Soldier Field. I was told that Vestee Jackson, one of the Bears defensive backs, had come up with a pick, but to this day I still haven't seen it. I just don't spend enough time on YouTube. In reality the second half of the Fog Bowl remains a blur, literally. Game plans changed because of such limited visibility.

"On punts, I told my guys not to block, not to block!" Dennis says. "I told them I wouldn't be out there because nobody could see me. I just stood on the sidelines with Ted Plumb until it was time for the offense to get back on the field."

I asked Dennis if he sought out Buddy Ryan before the ballgame. The game—much like Ali-Frazier—was billed a Ditka versus Ryan. I have a great deal of respect for Buddy.

"He scouted me," Dennis says. "He is probably the primary reason I wound up with Bears."

Speaking of which, shouldn't the Bears retire the number '85' in celebration of our Super Bowl Championship team? I know the club has retired a bundle of numbers going back to the halcyon days of Red Grange, Bronko Nagurski, and Sid Luckman, but there has to be room for at least one more number for the most dynamic team in NFL history.

"Our '85 team deserves it," Dennis says.

We never got around to this. As much as you beat Buddy in the Fog Bowl, the Bears beat Buddy in the historic—did you happen to see that play?—ballgame on the lakefront. A touchdown catch by Mike Quick was negated by a penalty and Keith Jackson, the tight end from Oklahoma, dropped a SURE TD pass in the end zone. I thought Buddy was going to flip out. Did you seek out either Mike or Keith after the ballgame to console them?

"Hell, no, I went to the locker room. We weren't like today's players. We didn't arrange to tweet about each other or plan a trip to Maui or the Bahamas. If we agreed to exchange jerseys, we would have either been fined or billed. Really."

After the game, Mike Ditka was chanting, bellowing that the road to the Super Bowl went through Chicago. Mike and the Bears had little time to gloat. The bedazzling San Francisco 49ers were coming to Chicago for the NFC Title game and a ticket to Super Bowl XXIII. I don't want to give away the narrative, but Joe Montana's QB rating in that match up was 136. The Bears were going to absorb an overhand right followed by a left hook to the body that rattled rib cages from Chicago to Carbondale and beyond.

Later that night, before 1988 gave way to 1989, a listless and lackluster member of the Bears, whose name is not worth mentioning, appeared on a New Year's Eve TV special on some local station. The big slug actually did his on-camera bit while holding and sipping an open bottle of booze. The kid presumably was dreaming dreams of being measured for a Super Bowl ring. Stay tuned.

###

I asked Dennis how badly he regretted having never played in a Pro Bowl. It has to hurt.

"I was phased out," Dennis says. "My blood still boils when I think about it. It reminds me of our Super Bowl win over the Pats. I scored nine touchdowns that season while Gault had three. Yet he was targeted all day by Jimmy Mac, while I got nothing. Jim threw my way once and the ball bounced in front of me. Guys on other clubs would tell me every year I belonged in the Pro Bowl. That tells me my peers knew the job I was doing and what I was putting out.

We had plenty of guys on our '85 title team that just didn't get the recognition they deserve. Take Emery Moorehead, a completely unselfish player, who always arrived ready to work. E wasn't like today's tight ends. He wasn't split five yards out, he lined up right next to a tackle, shoulder to shoulder, with a linebacker on top of him.

Emery just didn't make mistakes. He was completely reliable. Here again, in today's NFL where guys are building up numbers on seven- and eight-yard receptions, Emery could catch 55 or 60 balls a season The guy was blessed with remarkably soft hands.

This league has too many receivers today who catch around 90 balls a year who just run to a spot knowing where the ball is going to be. They average eight yards a catch and people think they're all world. There is no art in catching a ball like that. Receivers know they're free. They can't be hit, for gosh sakes, they can't be touched."

Today there's another thing that can't be touched. The check. Dennis grabs it, and we make arrangements for another afternoon in Northfield.

# Chapter Fourteen

I'm gazing at a website story listing the 25 greatest receivers in Bears history. The list had to be put together by some guy who began following the NFL around 2004. Harlan Hill, far and away the greatest receiver in Bears' history (in 1954-'56, playing 12 game schedules, Hill caught 32 TD passes and averaged about 23 yards a catch while always facing double-teams, sometimes triple-teams), is nowhere to be found.

Johnny Morris, a fleet-footed flanker, who set an NFL record for single season receptions with 103 in 1964, playing a 14-game schedule, is D.O.A., as is Ken Kavanaugh, a product of the Bears' legitimate "Monsters of the Midway" era back in the 40s. Kavanaugh, a superb athlete, had 50 career touchdown catches during a time when NFL teams were playing 11- and 12-game schedules.

Willie Gault is at the top of this ladder as Silk, ranked at nine on the list, begins to give the list a critical eye. Brandon Marshall turns up at 2 with Alshon Jeffrey at 3 and Marty Booker at 4.

"Devin Hester at five?" Dennis asks incredulously. "That's crazy, he was a return man. Curtis Conway at 6. He was just a possession guy. Johnny Knox at seven, how many years did he play in Chicago (three years before a devastating spinal injury ended his career)? Tom Waddle—8—a spot above me. Anybody who's ever followed the game knows I was a far more complete player on my worst day than Tom Waddle.

I want to know how Waddle made the All-Madden team (1991). That's B.S. The Madden list wasn't around when I played, but I know Madden appreciated the way I played the game, all sides of the game. Waddle on that list isn't laughable. It's out-and-out pathetic."

We talk about some other receivers in the league.

"Odell Beckham, blond hair, platinum hair, loves to talk about being a stud. He didn't even go after the ball on that onside kick against the Bears. I'm not surprised. He's always been a punk. His team needed him to make a simple play, and he punked out on his teammates. Shame on me, I thought football was a contact sport. I know Odell was pissed. (Giants running back) Saquon Barkley is the new golden boy in New York. He was getting all the ink. I guarantee you that just killed Beckham.

Beckham was afraid of contact on that squib. Here is what irritates me the most. A guy like Larry Fitzgerald at Arizona, one of the greatest wide receivers in NFL history, never gets the pub he deserves. The guy has 1,300 career catches or close to it (1,278). But a guy like Beckham is treated like the golden child. Odell's deal is worth just under 100 million dollars. 100 million and he looks at a live ball on an onside kick like a time bomb. Of course, Beckham will happily tell you anytime he is far and away the best receiver in the NFL."

After the game, Beckham, for all the world, actually appeared to be humble when he told the press he couldn't figure out why people would care about the onside kick. Odell didn't see any need to admit that he appeared to be scared half to death to go after the ball. He did mention that people could question him as a person but should never question his heart.

"Never question his heart?" Dennis says, sarcasm dripping. "Please, this guy has the audacity to tell people they shouldn't question his heart?"

What are Dennis's thoughts about former Bear Tom Waddle? I have an inkling of an idea, but I wanted to give an opportunity to elaborate.

"Some guy compared (former Bears wide out) Tom Waddle to me?" Dennis says, still thinking about that list of top Bears receivers. "That's an insult. Waddle had to struggle to make the team. He was just a guy who filled a roster spot. I put Lawrence Taylor on his ass on the Astroturf at Soldier Field. Waddle couldn't do that in his wildest dreams. He's relevant as a football player in the eyes of the public because he has his various broadcast platforms. Do you think Waddle would ever tangle with a guy like Ronnie Lott? Please, next case."

I asked Dennis to name his favorite possession receivers.

"When you talk about the great possession receivers of all time you have to talk about Charlie Joiner, Steve Largent, and Fitz. I can't just single out one as being the top guy. They all were great route runners, all were blessed with soft hands. None of them had blazing speed, but all got terrific separation coming out of the breaks. These guys were coaches' dreams—none were divas. Michael Irvin? He was a diva. Think about him walking into a Dallas courtroom in his full-length fur coat with oversized Hollywood shades."

Silky pauses before spewing more venom towards Dallas.

"The arrogance of the Cowboys starts with Jerry Jones. I played a year in Dallas after I left the Bears. Jimmy Johnson was the head coach. America's team, my ass. The 'Boys haven't been relevant for a decade and a half (last Super Bowl win—January 1996). Yes, they have the infamous Dallas Cowboy cheerleaders and their 'Jerry's World' Stadium, but the clubs they've packaged for their fans have, more often than not, been dysfunctional and inevitably disappointing.

Dallas gets way too much buildup. For example, I don't care how many more yards Emmitt Smith gained than Walter gained. Emmitt ran behind one of the greatest offensive lines in NFL history with guys like Nate Newton and Larry Allen. Plus, he was surrounded by skill with Troy (Aikman), Moose Johnston, Jay Novacek, and Irvin the ever-popular diva."

Walter joins the Bears in '75. He doesn't have a Pro Bowl O-lineman until 1983.

You ever see Emmitt throw a stiff arm like Walter? Forget it.

Smith played 14 years and rushed for just over 18,000 yards. Walter was on board 13 seasons and picked up 16,700 plus yards, but there is more to the story. Think about majestic ball carriers like Jimmy Brown, Barry Sanders, Adrian Peterson, Eric Dickerson, Edgerrin James, and Marcus Allen. They were all better running backs than Emmitt.

Emmitt was like Franco Harris at Pittsburgh, he had a free ride. How could Harris fail with those great O-lines Pittsburgh had back in the 70s?"

Since he was mentioned earlier, I asked Silky if he wanted to chime in on Devin Hester, the greatest return man the NFL has turned out since a young Gale Sayers.

"The Bears screwed up by trying to make Hester a wide out," Dennis says. "He just couldn't deal with contact. He couldn't block anybody. How many times do you recall him even being touched on punt and kickoff returns that went for six points? Now, once the Bears tried to make Devin a legitimate receiver, he couldn't handle it. Still, he was selected to the NFL's 2000s Team of the Decade and in an era of specialization, gadget players, he was simply in a class by himself. Devin wasn't used to getting hit. But he was making number one receiver money, so the Bears felt the need to justify what they were paying him. Hester didn't really run precise routes. He just used his speed. His wide receiver skills were limited."

###

We talk about some of the quarterbacks in the league, past and present. I always wondered where Silk came down on Jay Cutler, for instance.

"Jay Cutler was a gutless moron," Dennis proclaims. "His whole attitude was 'I don't give a fuck.' I wouldn't be surprised if his teammates hated him."

I asked him about Broadway Joe Namath.

"I'll tell you this," Dennis says. "(Joe) Namath doesn't go to the Hall of Fame if he doesn't win that Super Bowl. He's in the Hall of very good, much like a guy like Peanut Tillman, the ex-Bear. Tillman was a terrific player on a terrific defense with Mike Brown, Ted Washington, Robert "Tractor" Traylor, Lance Briggs, and Brian Urlacher. Briggs was a better overall player than Brian Urlacher, but the media made Urlacher the golden boy."

What about Matthew Stafford?

"He's never won a playoff game. He's making 27 million bucks this year. It amazes me just how much money people who define mediocrity can make in today's NFL."

Eli Manning?

"Eli looked pathetic against the Bears. He doesn't want the ball in his hands anymore. It's a bitch to say this about a guy who's won two Super Bowls, but Eli looked like a pussy versus the Bears. He's making $19,000,000 this year. You know the Giants would love to host a retirement news conference."

Aaron Rodgers' legacy will always be his ability to come up with 11th hour, Hollywood finishes to lift the Pack off the canvas. Where does Dennis stand on Rodgers?

"Think about the Seattle game in 2018," Silk says. "With a little under four minutes left, all Green Bay needed was a field goal and a defensive stand to win a big road game. Fourth and two and Aaron is your quarterback. Who do you trust, a second-rate defense or Rodgers, who's big play adrenaline had to be bursting from all pores? McCarthy chose to punt. He'd fucking rather kick than let a Hall of Fame quarterback try to pick up two yards. McCarthy was telling his guys you're worthless, I don't trust you."

Rodgers could have been forgiven for decking Mike. You don't have to be a genius to recognize that the schism between Rodgers and McCarthy reached a new level on that Sunday afternoon. Rodgers had to feel betrayed. You know the narrative from here. Green Bay couldn't put the clamps on the Seattle offense and Rodgers never got to touch the football. That was the end. The Pack could have mailed in the remaining dates on the schedule.

"McCarthy will regret that decision for years, a decision that ultimately had to lead him to losing his job. If the Packers had won versus the Rams and Seattle, they're still in the race instead of a club that looks hopelessly divided."

What about the wunderkind in Los Angeles?

"Let me bring this point up," Dennis says. "If my guy Richard Dent had lined up against Jared Goff when the Bears played the Rams, Goff might have left Soldier Field on a stretcher. Richard would have gone on a feeding frenzy. Dent would have smelled blood in the water. Goff looked like he was playing in Siberia. His hands were in his warmer all night. He looked like a guy who couldn't wait to get to the bench. Richard would have had Goff trembling on the sidelines. Jared was a sitting duck. I was surprised, make that shocked, that the Rams and Goff couldn't exploit the Bears' secondary. However, that can happen when you are looking at second and nine all night as the Rams were. Jared is like a lot of quarterbacks today. They panic. They don't know how to avoid a sack or escape the tackle box."

Silk is flying at 35,000 feet as the curtains drop on 2018, the year the Bears proved there could be life after three years of death by strangulation under John Fox. Silk is rolling. He's tossing out one-liners at such a furious pace I'm reminded of the classic rock anthem "Born to be Wild," turned out by John Kay and Steppenwolf 50 years ago. "Get your motor running dead out on the highway lookin' for adventure and whatever comes our way."

I ask him about the other quarterback in the Bears division, Kirk Cousins.

"We paid you 84 million bucks guaranteed for this shit?" Dennis says. "The Viks embarrassed themselves. Did you hear the way their fans were booing them? That can happen when it takes you twenty-six minutes to rack up a first down. Look at Cousins. He was pathetic. He made over 40 million bucks at Washington, now he's sitting on 84 million dollars in guaranteed money with Minnesota. Cousins is the kind of guy, and they're in abundance, who just doesn't want the ball in his hands when the glare of the spotlight is at its brightest.

In some regards he reminds me of Jim Harbaugh. You know Harbaugh and I got into it big time when he joined us in camp back in 1987. Jim was late on a read and his throw had me sitting like a duck out of water during a 7-on-7 drill after I'd beaten a defensive back. Keep in mind I'm coming back after a season lost because of my knee.

So, I go back and get in his face and tell him if you want to play on this level you've gotta be able to read the routes. Then I added, aren't you reading the fucking coverage? There was some pushing and shoving but no punches thrown. One of our offensive linemen, probably Jimbo Covert, broke up a very one-sided 'fight.' We had to be separated. You're damn right I won the so-called fight. (Mike) Ditka loved training camp fights. He'd sit in his Pope Mobile (golf cart) and laugh like crazy until he finally blew the whistle."

Since the subject of Harbaugh was broached, I pursued it. What did Silky really think of his former Bears quarterback?

"Harbaugh's been hiding behind smoke and mirrors all his life. When he joined us, all he could talk about was how great he was at Michigan. Somebody should tell the guy you can't hide anywhere when you lose your last two games this past season to Ohio State, a club you have never beaten, and Florida while giving up 103 points."

Were you as shocked as I was when Harbaugh told the press after the Wolverines lost to the Gators that he didn't plan on making any changes with his coaching staff?

"No. You can call your own shots, you don't have any worries, when you're on a guaranteed deal that runs through 2021. This'll kill you. His deal includes $250,000 in bonus money for winning a Big 10 title. I wonder if Ohio State knows that. My two NFL busts of the year are Cousins and Jon Gruden at Oakland. Jon's biggest league-wide contribution in 2018 came in making the Bears and Dallas instant hits by dealing Khalil Mack to Chicago and Amari Cooper to Dallas, where Cooper flourished with Ezekiel Elliott in the Cowboys' backfield.

Neither the Bears nor the 'Boys make the playoffs without the additions of Mack and Amari. The struggle was real for both Chicago and Dallas until those two guys showed up. 30 years from now some team will make two deals in one year as stupid as Gruden's, and football fans will say, 'Ya know what, those trades were as dumb as the moves that guy in Oakland made in 2018.'

The Vikings will be paying Cousins $29,000,000 during the final year of his contact. In other words, don't even think of cutting the loser because the cap hit would make you roadkill. A $500,000 workout bonus as part of his deal? When I played I didn't know what a workout bonus was."

I had been meaning to ask Dennis about a defensive player I knew he respected. This seemed like as good a time as any. What were Silky's thoughts about Derrick Thomas?

"You know Derrick also graduated from South Miami Senior High School, like I did. He was a little younger than I was, so we really never got to know each other…we were like two ships passing in the night. Let me tell you this about Derrick. You know how much I love Wilber Marshall. The greatest compliment I can give Derrick, the highest praise I can offer is this: Derrick had a quicker first step than Wilber. Derrick is too often left out of the conversation when people talk about great linebackers. D.T. went to nine Pro Bowls, he was a six-time All Pro, and he is a member of the NFL's 1990s Team of the Decade.

We lost Derrick when he was just 33 years old from a severe blood clot that brought on paralysis. If you're going to talk (Dick) Butkus, Lawrence Taylor, Junior Seau, or an old-timer like Ray Nitschke, you have to put Derrick on the same bus. He was just a razor blade in shoulder pads."

# Chapter Fifteen

Why did it take so long, so many years, for the team President Obama called the greatest in history to gaze at the Rose Garden? Go back to 1986, two days after the Bears had wiped the Superdome floor with Ray Berry and the Patriots 46-10. It might have been 46-13 if Bill Belichick had been guiding New England.

Yes, the '85 champs were scheduled to visit President Reagan at the world's most famous residence (includes bowling alley and basketball court and a swell movie theater) shortly after they won the title, but an unforeseen tragedy left America in mourning.

The space shuttle *Challenger*, launched from Cape Canaveral, crashed just 73 seconds into flight, landing in the Atlantic Ocean. All seven crew members aboard perished. Obviously, the administration had to make other plans for the Bears. In the name of patriotism, mourning and respect, the Bears' visit was pushed aside. Somehow, the team just never did get its trip to Washington D.C.

Many years went by, and while it would come up occasionally in conversation, the Bears' visit to D.C. just seemed to become like a busted hockey stick, something shoved away in the back of an attic.

"You know (Dan) Hampton didn't make the trip," Dennis points out. "He had stated he didn't like President Obama, but the reasons actually sink to a lower level. Hampton was a staunch Republican who didn't want to honor a black president."

Steve McMichael, one of Hampton's running mates, was critical of Dan's decision to blow off the White House. McMichael made it very simple pointing out that a person simply doesn't ignore the chance to visit the White House.

"You know Hampton's a drinker," Dennis says, "and when guys get too much to drink, they begin to spout, especially at banquets, golf outings, or when they're with their inner circle of friends. Word on comments made by Hampton had a way of trickling back through our locker room in Lake Forest. As teammates, we really didn't really discuss Hamp's views, we just knew what they were. There are a lot of things you mask, keep under wraps, knowing that as long as you can co-exist for the good of the common goal, things will somehow take care of themselves.

I want Dan Hampton to know this. Retired NFL players know he isn't in the Hall of Fame if Richard Dent doesn't arrive on the 8th round as part of our historic class of 1983 draft and free agency haul. I do know Hampton was disgusted when the Hall gave Richard his yellow blazer. You know a lot of our guys on defense were just bullies, they lived life like bullies. Hampton should be ashamed of himself, but bullies are never ashamed.

I have another issue with Dan Hampton. I'm sick of him bashing Jim McMahon. Give it up. Dan owes Jim an apology, but cowardice won't let Dan make that kind of move. I would tell Hampton no matter what you think about me, I'm still here."

I asked Silky if he spent any time in the West Wing or the Oval Office. He seems to have mastered the art of the photo-op. Dennis and Willie Gault practically camped out in Barack's breast pocket.

"No, we didn't get the full tour," Dennis says, laughing at my characterization. "I do recall Mr. Obama telling us, 'You can run in my house, but don't break any furniture.' You could tell, as a Chicago guy, that he was as thrilled to see us as we were to be in his company.

A degree of surrealism existed. I remember we were driven by police escort to the White House, where we zipped through security. I was thinking about all the movies I had seen where the White House was the backdrop. And, this may sound sentimental, but of course I was thinking about my mom and dad."

###

While many players leave town after their football careers end, Dennis has chosen to take up residency in Chicago. He remains busy as ever and is immersed in numerous charitable causes.

"People will say 'he has money,'" Dennis says, "'he should give back.' Celebrities are expected to give some of their money back to charity. They never served in the military. They didn't fight for their country. Shame on them for being selfish and cheap. Do it for the kids! We know they have free time.

I have worked with charities for over three decades. I've always tried to have a clear vision and purpose for giving of my time because it helps people in need. It does tug at your heart."

Dennis has given time, effort, and sometimes money to Boys and Girls Clubs, Boy Scouts of America, Illinois Pediatrics Brain Research Center, Chicago Public Schools, and as a member of the Board of Directors along with, among others, Paul Vallas, the former CEO of Chicago Public Schools.

"I have learned this about education. Without it, you're thrown in the water with sharks."

D.A.R.E, Gridiron Greats, the legendary Irv Kupcinet's Purple Heart Foundation, and the State of Illinois Organ Program run by Secretary of State Jesse White have all benefited from Dennis's presence.

Silky has also lent his name and time to the March of Dimes, Catholic Charities as a Board of Directors member, the Juvenile Diabetes Foundation, and the Dave Duerson Foundation to prevent alcohol and substance abuse.

"Where do you begin to express how you can help people in need and why you choose to help people in need?" Dennis asks. "I can tell you that giving and helping people is in my blood. Yes, certainly, some of it comes from how you were raised. But also seeing so much pain and suffering in the world should move you."

Silky has supported the Hines Veteran's Hospital, Share your Soles, NPH-USA, and the LaSalle County (Illinois) Farm Bureau Foundation Agriculture in classroom programs.

"Some days you have to sit down and reflect on your life. The journey is never easy, yet when you pause and reflect, a smile begins to emerge. I was born in a small town, Quitman, Georgia, but a rapid move to South Miami, Florida is where my journey really begins.

I was a kid with an effervescent smile who would become very good student-athlete. I was born to wonderful blue-collar parents who provided me with strict rules and guidelines. That's where my DNA was established."

Dennis has lent time to Shop with a Cop, served as a spokesman for Brown's Chicken, worked as spokesman for the State of Illinois' program to stop underage drinking. Note, Dennis told me he hasn't had a drink since he lost his dear pal Dave Duerson in 2009. Silk has also been on board with the Greater Chicagoland Food Depository.

And there's one institution he really helps—and it's a labor of love.

"Dr. Scott Kolbaba is a man I truly admire," Dennis says. "We have worked together at the Illinois Youth Center—St. Charles."

Scott will tell you, "Dennis's message is about respect, especially for your mother. When he speaks to these kids you can hear a pin drop. The kids clearly relate to Dennis. He is a tremendous role model."

In addition to having four biological children, Scott has adopted two kids from Romania and one from Chicago's south suburbs. He has also authored the bestseller *Physicians' Untold Stories: Miraculous Experiences Doctors Are Hesitant to Share with Their Patients, or Anyone!* The Doc also has a private medical practice which includes patient Dennis McKinnon.

Silk and Scott have been mentoring and educating at the St. Charles lock-up for the past year.

"Of course, we deal with 'O.G.s,' Original Gangstas," Dennis says. "There are too many kids who have been thrown away like trash, just forgotten about. All they do is talk to priests and pastors. Some will go years without seeing a family member.

I tell these kids I am a volunteer, I'm not getting paid to speak with them. I do my best to talk to the kids and not at them. We are trying to condition them for the outside. How can the Doc and I help them get a G.E.D, a place in the military, a job, and housing?

When I go into St. Charles, I don't have my driver's license or cell phone. I'm in their world. You really try as hard as you can to convince the kids to understand the importance of placing a value on life. It's not easy. The prison is not going to tell you a thing about the kids. You have to get through to kids who in many cases hate themselves.

They want to know, can they trust me? I frequently tell them that I'm a lottery ticket. I've worked hard my whole life, but I was lucky I had my football skills and other talents to find my place in society. These kids see society as an enemy.

Sometimes, you'll talk to five or six kids together. They're all going to jockey for position. They all want to be the alpha dog. I remind them of something they really aren't sure how to observe: freedom has its privileges. I tell them the facts. You have to be upfront with me, no employer is going to give you the time of day with an Equivalency Diploma.

No kid has ever tried to get rough with me. First off, there are guards around us and most of them have seen a few of my game tapes, which sends a message that I'm not the guy you wanna mess with.

Generally, the kids see the Doc and I as a breath of fresh air. Some kids will also ask the questions you might expect: Do I know Jerry Rice or Emmitt Smith; do I drive a Ferrari?

I give them this piece of advice. I don't care about a mixed-up world where you are 'Liked' on social media. The whole world is living on likes, which is just stupid. You want to be loved by those who matter.

Doc and I are working to fill the gaps in a misplaced system where the state has no resources left to help these young men once they are out of prison. It's tragic. Too many of these kids are battling depression, insomnia, and other bitter forms of mental stress. Two weeks out, they're left without the medication they need. You tell me that doesn't make them an easy mark for drug dealers.

The state has got to grant these young people proper medication, medication they deserve. It's just that simple. But everybody knows the kids inside are society's abandoned people. The Doc and I will never give up the battle for change inside and on the street.

That is just how we are."

### 

Let's get in the hurry up offense…Give me 10, 11, 12 things people may or may not know about Dennis McKinnon.

"Number 1. I'm a pretty good bowler. I average about 180, but I never practice.

2. I'm afraid of heights.

3. If I could only see one concert the rest of my life, I would love

to see the original Earth, Wind & Fire or Michael Jackson.

4. I absolutely cannot swim.

5. I briefly coached the legendary Chicago Bliss of the legendary Lingerie Football League. That lasted until I realized the team ownership had no plans to pay me. I even got a copyright on the playbook I drew up, which by the way contained a jet sweep. The lingerie league is a sham. They used my name to put the team together and my playbook to win the league's first title. Nothing like being exploited.

6. I am a movie buff. I love *To Kill a Mockingbird* and *The Shawshank Redemption*. Shawshank is a story of great friendship, but also a telling tale of maintaining faith when the devil is upon you.

7. My favorite vacation retreat is Jamaica. I love Montego Bay.

8. The NFL team I dislike the most has got to be the Dallas Cowboys. One, in my brief time with the Cowboys, they treated me miserably. That star at midfield has been dead for years.

9. I love TV drama. I'm not big on *Law and Order*, but I love shows that deal with forensics evidence—and force you to think. *NCIS* and *CSI: Crime Scene Investigation* are my favorites.

10. I will always miss the sessions I had with Walter Payton on the Saturday nights before Sunday ballgames. I will take those to my grave.

11. I am ambidextrous, but my right hand goes dead when I type. My left hand has to work overtime.

12. My favorite contemporary athletes include Mike Trout, Tiger Woods, Serena Williams, Steph Curry, and Lindsey Vonn. Think of what Lindsey's achieved and how much pain she's had to endure.

Game, set, and match.

# Acknowledgments

There so many people who have earned my love and respect. I know I can't mention them all, but those who know me know that they will always be in my heart.

Mom: All that I am today is built on the foundation you laid out for me. The basic values you taught me have earned me the love and respect of so many people. I love you and still miss you.

Virginia McCaskey: She is the silent one. I have so much respect for her. When I'm in her presence, I feel like I'm on holy ground.

Brian McCaskey: The one McCaskey brother I truly admire. Brian has always shown me nothing but love. Dare I say he is the finest of the McCaskey brothers?

Dave Duerson: I still cry over Double D leaving us so tragically. Several days ago, I was driving down Collins Avenue in Miami not far from where Dave lived when he took his own life. I just stopped my car and began to cry. It still pains me that I never had the chance to say goodbye to my brother.

Yvette Fuse: Yvette is so special. Just a wonderful woman. Dave was her uncle. When Double D took ill, she became the Rock of Gibraltar in the Duerson family. She handled everything and also served as a conduit with the family.

Wilber Marshall: The work he put in can never be denied. He is on my list of the 10 greatest defensive players I've ever seen, along with Lawrence Taylor, Reggie White, and Ronnie Lott. The NFL has conspired to keep him out of the Hall of Fame. Wilber, Walter, and Double D were my three best friends on the 80s Bears.

Kevin Butler: He had the mentality all great kickers have: "I don't give a fuck." I have a special love for Butt-Head since I was born in

Quitman, Georgia, and Kevin played for Vince Dooley and the Georgia Bulldogs during the Herschel Walker era. In the '85 draft we landed William Perry, but Kevin's arrival the same year may well have been the final piece we were missing. Nerves of steel. Defiant.

Buddy Ryan: His knowledge of football was significantly greater than Mike Ditka's level. I will never forget the fact that Buddy scouted me, and saw in me a guy who could succeed on the NFL stage.

Matt Suhey: Walter used to love to tease him. Matt was the personification of class. His drive and determination always reminded me of Robert Newhouse, the former Dallas Cowboy.

Les Frazier: So humble, so decent. He lined up and did his job to perfection. How many times do you recall Les getting beat on the deep ball? It was rare when he didn't win the downfield battle. Les and Double D covered a lot of ground that Gary Fencik just didn't have the tools to cover.

Ted Plumb: I called him the Gargamel, one of the Smurfs, because of his hair. There was an island of emptiness on the top of his head separated by streams of water on the sides of his head. Ted and I used to love to tease each other. Ted gave me respect, he pushed me. I love Ted Plumb.

Jay Hilgenberg: The strongest link in the chain along our offensive line. How does a guy who went to seven Pro Bowls not have a bust in Canton at the Hall of Fame? That really breaks my heart.

Emery Moorehead: Royal crown. I have nothing but love and admiration for E. Like so many players on our '85 Bears, he was pathetically underrated.

Jimbo Covert: My admiration for him is second to none. He was a first round pick on our historic 1983 draft class, a class which changed the culture of the Chicago Bears. He definitely rates with Anthony Munoz when the topic is great left tackles.

Willie Gault: Willie and I will always be brothers. No, we didn't always get along or agree on issues. I call that normal. Sometimes jealousy and betrayal were part of our relationship. That's all gone.

Walter Payton: Sweetness was never sour with me. He was a reflection of why we play the game we love. The Walter Payton Man of the Year Award is the highest honor a player can receive.

Ron Simmons (Billed as Farooq and Doom #1 among other names as a solid, villainous professional wrestler): He was a man among boys. He was my host on my visit to Florida State. I knew then I was important. The school wasn't going to have a second-rate player chaperone a guy they knew could help Florida State win. Ron Simmons was a stud, a consensus All-American in 1979 and again in 1980.

Johnny Roland: Reminded me of Grady Wilson from *Sanford and Son*. Truly a class act. He was the only black coach on our staff. Johnny was a no-nonsense coach who had the complete respect of Walter Payton.

Florida State: A great place to be a football-playing student athlete. You couldn't beat the climate, the girls, or the winning culture. The school opened the doors to my interest in criminology. You know Ted Bundy, the serial killer, murdered two women who attended FSU. Bundy was obviously a psychopath, but he was also, like most serial killers, something of a genius.

Marc Paskow: I love him like a father. I love his family. Coach Marc always had my back. Funny with a great presence. Marc may be Jewish, but there is some black blood flowing through his veins. His message to me was, "You have great talent, don't blow it."

Judy Keener: A loyal Bears fan. I don't think she's missed a game in 30 years. Judy served as my advisor when I got to Chicago. She advised me on how to handle community relations as well as the media.

Charles Kendrick, my old high school running mate at South Miami H.S.: He was "Red" and I was "Shotgun." Charles played tight end on our football team. We remain very close to this day. Charles will tell you, "Dennis worked so hard you thought he was the worst player on our team rather than the best."

Dave Duerson: One of the smartest guys I've ever known. We became brothers in 1983 as rookies with the Bears. Gone way too soon, but gone with a unique degree of class and dignity.

Mike Ditka: You can't say enough about Mike. He was the right coach at the right time for the Bears. Very demanding, very self-absorbed. Coach respected me a lot because I played tough and played through pain. But of greater importance, I made plays. I just wish Mike would have pushed to get me a bigger contract back in 1987.

And finally, thank you to the fans, my marketing team, Chet Coppock and my posse: Mike Taylor, Mike King, John Gikles for always having my back. Success is inevitable when the quality of the team and the product is exceptional. Chet and I have been friends for a very long time. I'm thankful that we finally got a chance to work on a project together about my life. We didn't agree on everything, but he did a masterful job on this book. I hope everyone puts this in their collection.

# About the Authors

*Dennis McKinnon*

Dennis is the founder and CEO of Bearly Active Productions Inc, an organization that connects corporations and charitable organizations with professionals in the sporting world. Because of his character and integrity, Dennis has forged unprecedented relationships with college leaders, professional football players (past and present), corporate executives, political leaders, and a vast amount of national charities.

Dennis played professional football with the Chicago Bears, Dallas Cowboys, and Miami Dolphins. He played under some of the most coveted coaches in NFL history: Mike Ditka, Jimmy Johnson, and Don Shula. Throughout his postseason career, Dennis has held many roles, including Executive Spokesperson, Director of Sponsorship, and Liaison to the NFL Retired Players with Gridiron Greats.

*Chet Coppock*

Chet Coppock has been broadcasting and writing about sports since he was a teenager. He was producer for the Milwaukee Bucks radio network, the sports director for WISH-TV in Indianapolis, lead sportscaster for Chicago NBC affiliate WMAQ-TV, and host of Cablevision's NewSportsTalk, before revolutionizing sports talk radio when he launched Coppock on Sports on WMAQ Radio in the 1980s. Chet passed away in April of 2019, just as we were preparing the book for publication.

Never a more charming lady--my beacon, my love, my mom.

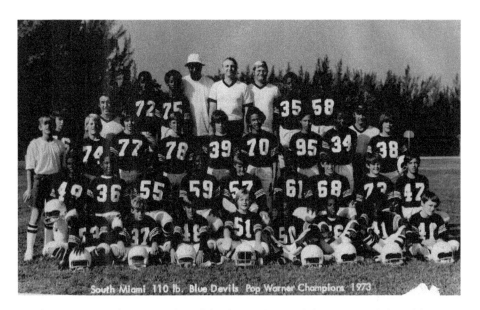

3rd row. I'm wearing 34--a sign of the future. Damn right we were unbeatable. We were so good we even had a sponsor.

Double dose of power and skill. McKinnons on both sides of the ball. Silky and Cousin Donald. I ditched my fro when it became too much to fit under my helmet.

A thrilling night playing high school football in the historic Orange Bowl.

Simply put, #22 on South Miami High School was a man among boys--one of the greatest football players in Florida history.

High school practice at night. That's Silky, far right.

Graduation Day FSU. My mom's dream had been realized.

Dad and my uncle Leonard McKinnon.

Coach Marc Pascow with his wife Susan and his wonderful daughters Lisa and Amy in the foreground. I love it when the girls call me Uncle Dennis.

Coach Marc's beautiful daughters Amy & Lisa

Professor Ted Plumb with his wideouts and tight ends

Congrats from Big Jim Covert and Jim McMahon after Mac and I hooked up on a TD strike in our 1985 playoff game against the Giants.

Always an "A-List" guest. Coppock with Silky at Mike Ditka's City Lights

Historic photo of the team taken at Deerfield High School while we
worked out during the 1987 players strike.

A meeting of '85 teammates at the legendary Cog Hill. It was cold as
hell--you can see me wearing gloves.

My brother Double D--Dave Duerson, and the outrageously flamboyant Mongo McMichael.

Talk about unlimited sex appeal. Holding court with Willie Gault and Otis Wilson.

Resort Travel International Time Share Company photo--Wilber Marshall, Mike Singletary, Otis Wilson, Dave Duerson, and Silky D.

My ad for Brown's Chicken

All's well that ends well. Willie Gault and I will always be linked.

With the wrestler, the Undertaker, Mark Calloway

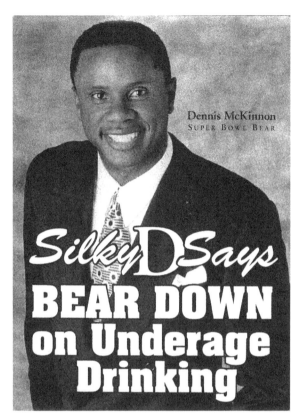

Late 80s, for the State of Illinois. I haven't had a drink since Dave Duerson died.

How many wrestlers in the Vince McMahon entourage had the impact
of Stone Cold Steve Austin?

The NFL's all-time leading rusher Emmitt Smith.
During my time in Dallas we were close.

Sure he can be a diva, but he was a majestic football player. Time spent with Michael
Irvin was always an experience.

Sharing laughter with Secretary of State Hillary Clinton

To: Dennis McKinnon

Best Wishes, Mayor Richard M Daley

I was on school board while Daley was in office.

Silky D, Willie Gault and Jim McMahon positioned for face time with President Obama during 2011 visit to the White House.

Silky D.